Global Perspective Seri

Integrity in Nigerian Politics

GLOBAL LIBRARY

This book is well written as it coherently articulates the moral issues prevalent in the Nigerian democratic system. No doubt, the work is one of the best texts composed with reference to biblical political ethics in several ways. It is sufficiently comprehensive, analytical, insightful, applicable, and practicable in the classroom and outside of it in scholarship engagements. This is an important book for everyone interested in Nigerian democratic ethos of biblical extraction.

Jacob K. Ayantayo, PhD
Professor of Religious Ethics, Religion and Society,
University of Ibadan, Nigeria

This highly readable book on Christian political ethics, which is focused on Nigeria, is well-thought through, insightful, well-researched, and distinctively evangelical in approach. It encompasses all that is necessary for African Christians, and indeed non-Christians in Africa, to understand ethical politics. It makes clear why the ultimate demand from God for politicians in Africa is integrity. This subject matter seems to be the major challenge in the African political process. This book challenges Nigerians in particular to think well and it provides the tools they need to serve in a God-honoring way in politics. The author articulates, and rightly so, that the man or woman who "has integrity must be of sound moral principle, honest and upright in conduct as well as in purity of the heart." The book presents itself in a way that students of ethics and political science will particularly appreciate.

Deji Isaac Ayegboyin, PhD
Professor of Religious Studies,
University of Ibadan, Nigeria
Visiting Professor,
Bowen University, Iwo, Osun State, Nigeria

Integrity in Nigerian Politics

An Introduction to Christian Political Ethics

GoodFriday N. Aghawenu

GLOBAL LIBRARY

© 2021 GoodFriday N. Aghawenu

Published 2021 by Langham Global Library
An imprint of Langham Publishing
www.langhampublishing.org

Langham Publishing and its imprints are a ministry of Langham Partnership

Langham Partnership
PO Box 296, Carlisle, Cumbria, CA3 9WZ, UK
www.langham.org

ISBNs:
978-1-83973-057-3 Print
978-1-83973-450-2 ePub
978-1-83973-451-9 Mobi
978-1-83973-452-6 PDF

GoodFriday N. Aghawenu has asserted his right under the Copyright, Designs and Patents Act, 1988 to be identified as the Author of this work.

All rights reserved. No part of this publication may be reproduced, stored in a retrieval system or transmitted, in any form or by any means, electronic, mechanical, photocopying, recording or otherwise, without the prior written permission of the publisher or the Copyright Licensing Agency.

Requests to reuse content from Langham Publishing are processed through PLSclear. Please visit www.plsclear.com to complete your request.

Scripture quotations, unless otherwise indicated, are taken from the Holy Bible, New International Version®, NIV®. Copyright ©1973, 1978, 1984, 2011 by Biblica, Inc.™ Used by permission of Zondervan.

Scripture quotations marked (NLT) are taken from the Holy Bible, New Living Translation, copyright © 1996, 2004, 2007, 2013, 2015 by Tyndale House Foundation. Used by permission of Tyndale House Publishers, Inc., Carol Stream, Illinois 60188. All rights reserved.

Scripture quotations marked (NASB) are taken from the New American Standard Bible®, Copyright © 1960, 1962, 1963, 1968, 1971, 1972, 1973, 1975, 1977, 1995 by The Lockman Foundation. Used by permission.

Scripture quotations marked (TLB) are taken from The Living Bible copyright © 1971. Used by permission of Tyndale House Publishers, a Division of Tyndale House Ministries, Carol Stream, Illinois 60188. All rights reserved.

Scripture quotations marked (NKJV) are taken from the New King James Version (NKJV). Copyright © 1982 by Thomas Nelson, Inc. Used by permission. All rights reserved.

British Library Cataloguing-in-Publication Data
A catalogue record for this book is available from the British Library.

ISBN: 978-1-83973-057-3

Cover & Book Design: projectluz.com

Langham Partnership actively supports theological dialogue and an author's right to publish but does not necessarily endorse the views and opinions set forth here or in works referenced within this publication, nor can we guarantee technical and grammatical correctness. Langham Partnership does not accept any responsibility or liability to persons or property as a consequence of the reading, use or interpretation of its published content.

Contents

	Introduction	ix
	Abbreviations	xv
1	The Concept of Morality, Politics, and Integrity	1
	Morality and Ethics	2
	Politics and the Bible	4
	Integrity in Politics	10
	Characteristics of Integrity in Politics	14
	Biblical Characters of Integrity	22
	Conclusion	28
2	Politics in Relation to Ethics and Religion	29
	Politics and Ethics	32
	Moral Values in Politics	33
	Politics and Religion	35
	Conclusion	42
3	A Historical Survey of Nigerian Political Society	43
	Pre-Colonial Politics in Nigeria	44
	Colonial Politics in Nigeria	48
	Formative Years of Modern Nigeria	49
	Independence Politics in Nigeria	54
	Military Politics in Nigeria	60
4	New Era of Democratic Politics in Nigeria	73
	Inter-Testament Democratic Politics in Nigeria	73
	New Era of Democracy in Nigerian Politics	76
	Moral Issues in the Nascent Democratic Politics	82
5	Moral Bankruptcy in Nigerian Politics	89
	Causes of Moral Bankruptcy in Nigerian Politics	89
	Effects of Moral Bankruptcy in Nigerian Politics	100
	Conclusion	107
6	Inculcation of Integrity into Nigerian Politics	109
	Politicians and Integrity	110
	Political Parties and Integrity	118

	Role of the Nigerian Government	121
	Responsibility of the Electorates	129
	Enhancement of Public Opinion	135
	Christians and Nigerian Politics	138
7	The Way Forward in Nigerian Politics.	141
	New Orientation on the Political Process	142
	Godly Leadership in Nigerian Politics	143
	Theocentric Approach to Political Life	146
	Bibliography	149

Introduction

Democratic politics has come to occupy a pivotal position in Nigeria's government today. Political activities are playing increasing roles in the shaping of individuals and culture. Significant decisions which are determining the destiny of the people of Nigeria are being made, not so much in the religious realm, as in the political process at the local, state, national, and global levels. Nigerian Christianity seems to drag its institutional feet on the most crucial issues of our day while political forces have moved in to right the social wrongs in the society.[1] The moral issues posed by Nigeria's democratic political processes are far too crucial for any serious religious person to ignore.[2] Thus, this book is an attempt to proffer solutions from the perspective of biblical Christianity, that is, to apply the biblical revelation[3] of political ethics to one of the pressing issues of the day – the moral bankruptcy in Nigerian politics.

The present level of integrity in Nigeria's democratic politics is very low. Integrity as an ethical or moral virtue is essential to any system of government. But this has been neglected in Nigerian government, hence, integrity is lacking in the governance of the day. Historically, the attitudes and practices of Nigerian political leaders, politicians, and their disciples, whether military or civilian, reveal a long and startling episode of unethical political practices.

Most contemporary Nigerian politicians and leaders are engaging in various vices such as falsehood, murder, infidelity, disloyalty, cheating, stealing, and all manner of corruption in the name of democratic politics. Political ruffians, thugs, vandals, arsonists, and assassins are the order of the day. Integrity is no longer viewed as an essential value. Politics is seen by many Nigerians as the quickest way to make money and to become popular. Thus, to grab political power becomes a do or die affair.

Many successive governments in Nigeria have shown concern about the declining moral ethos by launching various ethically orientated programs such as the Ethical Revolution (in 1983), the War against Indiscipline (WAI, in 1984), the Mass Mobilization for Economic Recovery, Self-Reliance and Social Justice (MAMSER, in 1987), the War against Indiscipline and Corruption

---

1. Barnette, "Protestants and Political Responsibility," 299.
2. Simmons, "Morality: Church and Government," 131.
3. Stott, *Issues Facing Christians Today*, xi.

(WAIC, in 1994) and the Obasanjo War against Corruption (WAC, in 1999). These programs yielded no results because their initiators themselves did not abide by the tenets of the programs.[4] Thus, the issue of integrity in national politics demands urgent attention. It is a striking indictment on our political system because many of our politicians cannot lead by example and therefore cannot promote high ethical standards and a sound moral ethos.

This negligence has generated some socio-ethical problems that demand academic research. This research work is in pursuance of the view that an academic enquiry should be carried out on the issue of the neglect of integrity as it relates to, or affects, Nigerian politics based on biblical Christianity, especially in the face of the failure of policy options as enumerated above.

The purpose of this study is threefold: first, the study exposes the Nigerian democratic society, political leaders, and politicians to the *biblical concept of integrity* in political ethics. Thus, this book examines the meaning of ethics, politics, and integrity from the biblical perspective, proving to Nigerians that integrity as a moral behavior is naturally and inevitably a vital element in practical politics. Integrity as it relates to politics is paramount in as much as it involves human happiness – "the good life" according to Aristotle;[5] second, the study sensitizes the citizens of Nigeria to the adverse effects of the *neglect of integrity* in Nigerian democratic politics. Thus, this book assesses the present democratic politics and examines the issues, causes, and effects of moral neglect in contemporary politics. The ongoing democratic politics in Nigeria is morally bankrupt. The book establishes the fact that the neglect of integrity is one of the major causes of aggression, hostility, cruelty, violence, bitterness, and the reckless destruction of human lives and properties that are occasionally experienced in our national politics.[6] This is because the lack of integrity is a fault line in the character that jeopardizes all other political values and undermines all human relationships.[7] No political action or reaction will be purposeful or effective if such steps are morally bankrupt; thirdly, the study shows *how to administer or restore integrity* into Nigerian democratic politics. It develops integrity in various aspects of national political life: the politicians, political parties, governments, and electorates as well as the Christian faith. The development of integrity is imperative in the democratic politics in

---

4. Ayantayo, "Comparative Study of Eschatology," 29.
5. Strang, "*Ethics as Politics*," 274–285.
6. Dzunrgba, *Nigerian Politics and Moral Behaviour*, viii.
7. McQuilkin, *Introduction to Biblical Ethics*, 381.

Nigeria. Biblical insights are carefully explored to help to promote integrity in Nigerian politics.

This area of study is significant because politics is one of the most basic and influential societal units in the world. Therefore, in the democratic governance of any nation like Nigeria, morality and ethics are indispensable. It is impossible to practice successful participatory democratic politics without moral integrity. A successful management of people, economic resources, funds, labor, authority, and power depends on the integrity or moral consciousness of the citizens.[8] Unless all Nigerians are "morally responsible and accountable for their words and deeds or utterances and actions the constitution, the law, human rights and freedoms, electoral process and legislation will not be meaningful in practical politics."[9] Thus, this study on integrity will contribute to cleansing and improving the political perception, thought, and moral behavior of the citizens of Nigeria. Hence, it will help to promote responsibility, accountability, and stability in Nigerian politics.

This work is also meaningful because it stimulates moral growth in practical politics in Nigeria. Ethical principles provide the standard by which one can measure his or her own moral development. In the light of this moral standard the individual may see what his or her political actions and reactions ought to be in terms of what he or she is actually doing.[10] This creates a tension and a discontent during our politicking toward the goal of perfection which God demands of Nigeria.

Another area of significance in this study is that it provides an *introduction to Christian political ethics* which gives more attention to the character of God as the pivotal point of successful politics than is usually given in current texts on the subject. Those who have had little or no orientation in biblical politics will find the work helpful. This book establishes the fact that the "Prime Mover" of human governance and his divine moral principles cannot be shelved in the politics of any country.

This enquiry is also relevant because of the intention to disarm the campaign for the autonomy of ethics and politics by the secular humanistic movement, which has already influenced Nigerian political activities. Humanistic ethics has denied any reference to God when crucial moral decisions are being made. This has given birth to the belief in the autonomy of moral standards and the autonomy of humans as moral agents. Humanists accept moral standards for

---

8. Dzurgba, *Nigerian Politics and Moral Behaviour*, xi.
9. Dzurgba, xi.
10. Barnette, *Introducing Christian Ethics*, 10.

their own sake but reject theological ethics. Humanism believes that one does not need religion in order to recognize cruelty.[11] Religion is irrelevant, and humans as mature moral agents, therefore, need no divine help in knowing what is right or wrong, valid or invalid, good or bad, in practical politics. This study, therefore, offers insight into the reality and relevance of religious ethics in politics in the twenty-first century. The world around us is constantly changing and those in the affairs of governance are constantly forced to make moral decisions in complex situations. Hence, in this moral struggle, they need all the socio-ethical insight possible in the light of biblical Christianity. This makes the study relevant and significant because it intends to foster the socio-ethical principles that will be of help to our nascent democracy.

Some schools of thought feel that Christianity is "too sacred" to be injected into politics.[12] Opinion polls continue to show that for a large majority of Nigerian citizens, politics is seen as a "dirty game." This book proves that this political "dirtiness" is really nothing but an unfortunate caricature which should be challenged. Politics is essentially an organized way of making corporate decisions in the affairs of any nation. There is nothing inherently dirty or unholy about that.[13] This is a meaningful contribution and an additional significance of this study, as the work challenges apolitical Christians to participate in political decisions with Christian moral principles and as citizens who have the right to lead.

Finally, this book is relevant because of the contribution it makes to scholarship and the opportunity it provides for the propagation of the will of God as far as political ethics is concerned. This will be seen by arousing the emotional, intellectual, and spiritual consciousness of readers to the principles and practice of the biblical concept of moral integrity in Nigerian politics.

The method applied in this study is a combination of library and field research, that is, an analysis of literary research method and interviews. The sources from the library have been used to present the biblical principle on integrity as it is related to the political process. This also implies application of literary analysis of some biblical verses to rectify the issue of moral failure in Nigerian politics.

As for the field work, although it was informal, participant observation, content analysis, and direct interviews greatly influenced this work. Unstructured observation was made on the trend of political activities taking

---

11. Abogunrin, "Religion and Ethics," 5.
12. Barnette, *Introducing Christian Ethics*, 161.
13. Tillman Jr., *Understanding Christian Ethics*, 127.

place in the Niger-Delta area through visits, interaction, and participation in the last local government election. Some radio and television programs were listened to in order to discern the political atmosphere and feelings of Nigerians with regard to moral failure in politics. Some eminent politicians and Christians were also interviewed, all within the Delta State of the Niger-Delta political zone.

Since the study is mainly on the ongoing civilian administration, our moral analysis may be viewed as current political affairs. Thus, the study methods have relied mainly on logical reasoning, keen observation, radio and television broadcasts, magazines, newsletters, bulletins, and other means such as discussions and chats. All these constituted the method of data collection. These research methods collaborated and complemented one another in diverse manners. Hence, the uniqueness of these methods of data collection, and the complexity of the pieces of information collected, have made it difficult for the author to acknowledge all the sources in detail. Therefore, a general taxonomy of sources has been considered as sufficient for this study. As a result, only a few cases will be acknowledged appropriately.

The scope of this research mainly covers the contemporary Nigerian democratic politics of Obasanjo administration from its inception in 1999 to the year 2004. The study will also make a brief historical survey of the political and moral issues and events that have taken place from pre-colonial politics to post-independence democratic politics. But the primary concern of this study is to assess the issues, causes and effects of the moral bankruptcy in the ongoing nascent democracy, especially in the Obasanjo junta. This period marks a new beginning of democratic political experiment in Nigerian democratic society after a long period of military interference in politics.

The thesis of this inquiry is that *there is moral bankruptcy in Nigerian politics* and *there is need to instill moral integrity based on biblical Christianity in order to make the political process a viable one*. In other words, if we are to find our way and play a constructive role in the political dialogue of our time, there is a need to understand the concept of integrity, and to develop a religious ethic that can propel integrity forward in a way that can be applicable to the current political situation in Nigeria. In order to achieve this, the work is divided into seven chapters following this introduction. The first chapter deals with the concept of morality, politics, and integrity. Chapter 2 deals with the how politics relates to ethics and religion. The third chapter presents a historical survey of Nigerian political society. Chapter 4 takes a close look at the nascent democratic politics in Nigeria that is the first tenure of Obasanjo administration. Chapter 5 assesses the moral bankruptcy in Nigerian politics.

The sixth chapter discusses how to inculcate integrity into Nigerian politics, and chapter 7 is the conclusion with recommendations for the way forward in Nigerian politics.

This book asserts that the Christian community has what it takes to infuse integrity into Nigerian politics through her teachings. Nigerian political history has been a history of perpetual conflict and bloodshed. But Christians, as citizens, have the divine mandate to inspire a revolution of morality and ethical behavior in Nigerian politics. Nigerians need new orientation on what democratic politics is all about; there is great need for more clear-sighted, courageous, and dedicated godly men and women in leadership; and there is need for a God-centered political process that is characterized by divine holiness, justice, and love to be valued equally by all Nigerians. It is the hope of this author that this work on Christian political ethics will be a boost to Nigerian democratic politics and also help to improve the moral situation of the country and the rest of the African nations.

Abbreviations

ANNP	All Nation Progressive Party
AD	Alliance for Democracy
AG	Action Group
AIG	Assistant Inspector-General
APP	All Peoples Party
BWAC	Berlin West Africa Conference
CCT	Child Care Trust
FEDECO	Federal Electoral Commission
FIFA	Federation of International Football Associations
GIFMIS	Government Integrated Financial Management and Information System
GNPP	Great Nigerian Peoples Party
GRA	Government Reservation Area
ICPC	Independent Corrupt Practices Commission
INEC	Independent National Electoral Commission
ING	Interim National Government
IPPIS	Integrated Payroll and Personnel Information System
MAMSER	Mass Mobilization for Economic Recovery, Self-Reliance and Social Justice
NADECO	National Democratic Coalition
NAFDAC	National Agency for Food and Drug Administration and Control
NCC	Nigeria National Constitutional Conference
NCNC	National Congress of Nigerian Citizens
NEC	National Electoral Commission
NECON	National Electoral Commission of Nigeria
NGO	Non-Governmental Organization
NPC	Northern People's Congress
NPN	National Party of Nigeria
NPP	Nigerian Peoples Party

NRC	National Republican Convention
OPC	Oodua People's Congress
PDP	Peoples Democratic Party
PRP	Peoples Redemption Party
SDP	Social Democratic Party
TSA	Treasury Single Account
UPN	Unity Party of Nigeria
WAC	War against Corruption
WAI	War against Indiscipline
WAIC	War against Indiscipline and Corruption
WOTCLEF	Women Trafficking and Child Labour Eradication Foundation

1

The Concept of Morality, Politics, and Integrity

Moral integrity is vital in Nigerian politics if we are to redeem our poor global image damaged in the past and present. In 1995, for instance, Ken Saro-Wiwa and eight other Ogoni people were sentenced to death by hanging, a sentence executed immediately by Abacha's administration. This coincided with the meeting of the Heads of State of the Commonwealth in Australia. The news of the hanging enraged the Heads of State meeting and Nigeria was expelled from the Commonwealth with immediate effect. Thus, our national image was badly tarnished and spoiled worldwide. Ironically, at the time of Nigeria's expulsion from the Commonwealth, its Secretary-General was Chief Emeka Anyaoku, a Nigerian from Anambra State. What an embarrassment from his own nation! There was international mockery, scorn, and contempt against Nigeria, "the giant of Africa," and her citizens. It was that same year, 1995, that Nigeria lost its hosting right for the World Cup Soccer Championship, changed from "Nigeria '95" to "Qatar '95," by the Federation of International Football Associations (FIFA).

We have lost many lives and much property, and will lose much more until Nigeria takes the wise decision of prescribing the right method of governance. The sanctity of human life should underlie Nigerian politics. We need to uphold, improve, and maintain the dignity, honor, integrity, and moral decency of politics. Thus, there is need to explain some operative terms for the sake of clarity in order to understand the thought pattern of this work. These are *morality* (ethics), *politics*, and *integrity*. Others will be defined when necessary in the body of the study. This is necessary because of the misconceptions some Nigerians have about politics and morality.

Morality and Ethics

The word *morality* simply means *the beliefs or ideas concerning what is right and wrong*, and how an individual should behave, whether good or bad, correct or incorrect, valid or invalid. It is what the society accepts as the standard of behavior, which every citizen should conform to.[1] Thus, every political action has social implications because it not only affects the politician but also the entire society. The society is the social background of moral acts. Based on this, a political action is accordingly judged as good or bad, and honest or dishonest, by the community.

In the same vein, judgement on any political activity is given in relation to how a particular behavior conforms to, or deviates from, the moral values of the society. "Moral values" means certain traits, characteristics, and virtues, such as integrity, honesty, justice, honor, purity, goodness, kindness, discipline, and trustworthiness, to mention a few. Moral values connote moral goodness, positive moral principles, moral strength, and the moral tone, which form the nucleus of the community's norm of morality.[2] It is expected that these moral values must be applied in the realm of socio-political arena in the society. On the other hand, non-conformity to moral values constitutes moral vices, which include injustice, dishonesty, partiality, nepotism, tribalism, corruption, inhumanity, scandal, anger, envy, lack of principles, lack of scruples, and others. It is expected that politicians should abstain from moral vices. Thus morality is a socio-political enterprise. It is used as an instrument of society that cuts across every facet of human relationship including politics.

Closely related to morality in meaning is the word *ethics*. The English word "ethics" is the anglicized form of the Greek, "ethical," which comes from *ethos*, meaning that which relates to character. Aristotle, the ancient Greek ethicist, opined that "ethical" is derived directly from *ethos*, which means "custom" or "habit." The presence of these two words, morality and ethics, in the English language reflects the dual Greek and Latin heritage.[3] Morality involves the actual living out of one's beliefs while *ethics entails more of how people ought to live out their life*. Ethics might be called a system of moral values and duties. It is concerned with the ideal human characteristics and actions. The study of ethics seeks to answer questions such as what ought a person do or refrain from doing? What attitudes of behavior should be viewed as good? And why

---

1. Ayantayo, "Comparative Study of Eschatology," 30.
2. Ayantayo, 31.
3. Grenz, *Moral Quest*, 23.

should they be considered good? What is the highest good, the chief end of human beings, the purpose of human existence?[4]

"Ethics is theology in action"[5] and political life is one of the valleys of action in human activities in society. From a Christian perspective, "ethics deals with what is morally right and wrong for a Christian"[6] living in any society. Grenz sees ethical living for a Christian to mean "ordering one's steps in every situation of life in accordance with the fundamental faith commitments."[7] These commitments are central for God. In other words, ethical living for godly persons entails being conscious of what they believe about God, oneself, and the world, and then acting according to the basis of these convictions. Therefore, one can ask the foundational ethical questions on political life: What does it mean to live according to our Christian faith commitments in this political situation? What response in this political context would be most in keeping with who God is, who we are, and what God's purpose is? To show why this is the case and what this means in political activity is the goal of this book. "Morals" and "ethics," however, will be used inter-changeably.

Ethics and morality work towards a decent political behavior and are vital tools in exposing corrupt practices and related offences in the public and private sectors of any given society. In this vein, in 2000, Obasanjo's civilian government established the Independent Corrupt Practices Commission (ICPC) by legislation. The ICPC was commissioned with the responsibility of investigating allegations of corrupt practices, immoral and criminal intrigues, manipulations, plots, and conspiracies in both low and high places in the public and private sectors of Nigerian society.[8] The main objective of the ICPC was to assist the government in an effort to reduce and perhaps end corruption and injustice in Nigerian politics.

Obasanjo's ICPC program encourages patriotic Nigerians to work toward decent moral behavior in Nigerian politics. For instance, Mrs. Margaret Icheen, the female Speaker of the House of Assembly in Benue State, brought some members of the House of Assembly to court on grounds of mismanagement of the assembly's funds which these politicians shared among themselves. But she was also accused of mismanagement of the assembly's funds, so the moral crisis worsened to the extent that the lawsuit instituted at Makurdi, the capital

---

4. McQuilkin, *Introduction to Biblical Ethics*, ix.
5. Grenz, *Moral Quest*, 20.
6. Grenz, 20.
7. Grenz, 20.
8. Dzurgba, *Nigerian Politics and Moral Behaviour*, 104.

of Benue State, was made null and void, and had no effect. At the peak of the political/financial crisis, the speaker, Mrs. Icheen resigned from office.

Nigerian women across the nation gave Mrs. Margaret Icheen their massive moral support for fighting corruption, most especially being the only woman speaker in Nigerian politics. Mrs. Icheen stood for decent political and moral behavior, and fought her political battle gallantly. She preferred to resign from her position as speaker than to compromise her moral integrity. Nigeria needs more women like her in democratic politics.

Politics and the Bible

Politics, as a word, means many things to many Nigerians. It is hard to explain exactly what politics means; however, a provisional explanation is necessary in our present discussion. Broadly speaking, *politics* is the organized conduct of relationships in any form of human community. It denotes the life of the city and community and the responsibilities of the citizens. Thus, it is concerned with the whole of our life in human society. "Politics is the art of living together in a community."[9] Narrowly speaking, however, politics is the government of human society in the state. It is the study of the ways in which a country is governed.[10] Politics will be applied here in its narrow sense, that is, politics as *a science of human governance.* In other words, politics here means the study of the ways in which Nigeria is governed, that which has to do with the regulating, conciliation, and reconciling of the diverse range of interests which occur within Nigeria's government. It is also about gaining power for social change.

Politics deals with power relations in a social context.[11] Politics takes place in a world organized into communities, institutions, and states in which men and women possess power and authority, maintain order, and so on. Politics concerns the behavior of groups and individuals in matters that are likely to affect the course of government, such as in voting, in forming and running political parties, or in exerting influences in other ways on those responsible for the conduct of government.[12] In other words, there is politics when people who have differential access to power (and authority) relate to one another in a society. It involves the struggle to share or distribute power, or the struggle to make authoritative (policy) decisions.

---

9. Stott, "Human Rights and Human Wrongs," 27.
10. Stott, *Issues Facing Christians Today*, 34; Bauckham, "Politics," 669.
11. Otite and Ogionwo, *Introduction to Sociological Studies*, 128.
12. Okolo and Ogionwo, 128.

In Otite and Ogionwo's view, "politics affects the private life of members of the society concerned."[13] This is because political action could be concealed, or it could be obvious, and it could involve the use of force to achieve its agenda. Although politics involves the opposition of groups or persons in the determination or exercise of power, it is also the organization of the total society and maintaining its integrity and boundaries. Order is maintained in society because those who exercise power and make rules are obeyed.[14] In other words, politics is human action governed by rules and standards of property and success; it is concerned with how political organizations actually work and about the casual connections between forms of institutions; it is also concerned with the types of politics likely to be pursued, or between structure and political power.

Politics Originated from the Heart of God

God initiated politics and entrusted it to humankind at creation. Politics is not a human invention as some people think. Therefore, for a proper understanding of the meaning of politics, there is need to examine it from a biblical perspective. It is believed that politics is embedded in the Genesis account:

> Then God said, "Let Us make man in Our image, according to Our likeness, and let them rule over the fish of the sea and over the birds of the sky and over the cattle and over all the earth, and over every creeping thing that creeps on the earth." God created man in His own image . . . God blessed them; and God said to them, "Be fruitful and multiply and fill the earth, and subdue it, and rule over . . ." (Gen 1:26–28 NASB)

It is explicit in this record that God initiated the idea of politics. He created humankind in his image and transferred the political tools and power to them in order that they could govern the earth with all integrity. Thus, politics has been given by God to enable man to govern the universe.

Political tools and moral abilities are embedded in the image of God in human beings – they are inherent in human nature. They are the religious and moral values for human political activities. In other words, God has given men and women wisdom, power of choice, power of management, power of love, the skill of judgement, and creative power. These are religious political tools given

---

13. Otite and Ogionwo, 128.
14. Otite and Ogionwo, 128.

to humanity at creation to enable them to govern the earth successfully. Thus, God establishes a political relationship between himself and his creation – God becomes the executive while men and women are the administrators. God expects his creatures to depend on him for a successful socio-political relationship. Politics is a network of relationships, which includes competition, clash of interests, compromise, cooperation, and consensus. Politics concerns itself not only with the conditions and consequences of human interactions, but also with actions and reactions; these are possible in God-centered politics.

Edenic Political Covenant

Critical studies of God's covenants with humankind in the Old Testament show numerous socio-political relationships. The first political covenant was established in the garden of Eden (Gen 2:15–17). The Edenic political covenant was given to Adam and Eve. They were charged to take care of the garden of Eden and to refrain from eating from "the tree of the knowledge of good and evil" (2:17 NASB). In other words, what God demanded from them was absolute obedience. Thus, politics is a divine relationship between God and human on one hand, and between human and fellow human on the other hand.

Adamic Political Covenant

The Edenic relationship was terminated by human disobedience when they ate the forbidden fruit. This failure led to the establishment of the Adamic political covenant with certain conditions that were to govern the life of human beings until the curse of sin would be lifted (Gen 3:14–21).[15] The socio-political power-tussle of the ages is predicted – a conflict between divine government and satanic government, or God-centered politics and humanistic politics (Gen 3:15). The Adamic regime was characterized by a broken relationship between the executive arm of the government (God) and the administrative arm of the government (human beings) on one hand, and the increase of moral decadence among human beings in world governance on the other hand. This moral depravity led to the destruction of the earth by the flood (Gen 7:1–24; cf. Ps 36:1–12).

---

15. The Open Bible, *New American Standard*, 5.

Noahic Political Covenant

God established the third political covenant with Noah after the flood (Gen 9:1–9). In the Noahic political relationship, God still maintained his original plan of human management of the earth, but he added the ethical principle of human governance, which included the responsibility of suppressing the outbreak of sin and violence. This was a new system of moral law and government, together with penalties for crime (9:1–6). God established the sacredness of human life because he knew that human civilization would definitely need some form of restraint and moral norms to protect citizens' lives (9:6).[16] The issue of the sacredness of life prompted the late Prof. Dora Nkem Akunyili into action to save lives in Nigeria. She was the Director-General of the National Agency for Food and Drug Administration and Control (NAFDAC) in Obasanjo's administration from 2001 to 2008. "After the death of her sister, Vivian, who died after taking [a] fake insulin injection in 1988, Dora came at the forefront of the battle against drug counterfeiters in Nigeria."[17]

Nigerian politics needs more patriotic women like Dora Akunyili – women of honesty and integrity, dedicated to service. She earned over 900 awards in her lifetime, including the Integrity Award 2003 by Transparency International. She is among eighteen women who have helped shape Nigerian politics since 1960. Despite the corruption of her day, Dora Akunyili lived blamelessly before Nigerians in the same way that Noah pleased God and walked blameless with him (Gen 6:9).

Abrahamic Political Covenant

But Noah's era was characterized by a total failure as well. Humankind revolted against the leadership of God and expressed their freedom by making their own gods. So, God decided to choose a man and make a nation out of him – a political model to transform all nations of the world. Thus, he established the Abrahamic political covenant. This is the first theocratic covenant God made with humanity. It is unconditional, dependent on God's grace, with the many declarations of "I will" (12:1–3).[18]

---

16. The Open Bible, 11.
17. Wikipedia, "Dora Akunyili," https://en.wikipedia.org/wiki/Dora_Akunyili.
18. The Open Bible, 14.

Israel's Political Covenant

Finally in the Old Testament era, God re-established a theocentric government with Israel as a fulfilment to his promise to Abraham. It is an Israelite political covenant (Exod 19:5–8). The political relationship was conditional on two things: faith and obedience. In other words, Israel had to remain *faithful* to God and *obedient* to his rules for governance.

In Israel's theocracy, God used Moses, Joshua, the judges, the prophets and prophetesses, and the kings as the intermediaries through whom he governed. Theocratic rule was also given, but Israel failed as a chosen nation,[19] when they demanded a king to rule them like the other ungodly nations around them. Israel thought of religion as a hindrance to their political development. They rejected God in their political affairs (cf. 1 Sam 8:4–9). Thus, they deviated from the original meaning of politics – *God-centered* politics.

In the New Testament era, we see the consequence of Israel's rejection of theocracy. Israel, a chosen nation who ought to be "a kingdom of priests and a holy nation" (Gen 19:6), was subjected to the godless civil politics of an unholy nation – the Romans. This political slavery led to Israel's anticipation of a "political messiah" promised by God in the Adamic era. They anticipated the day when the sons of light would utterly crush the sons of darkness.[20]

We may ask whether Jesus is a political messiah, or whether he is involved in politics. From the expectation of the Israelites, he is not. In this sense, according to John Stott, "he never formed a political party, adopted a political program, or organized a political protest. He took no step to influence the policies of Caesar, Pilate, or Herod. On the contrary, he renounced the then-known political career."[21] But if politics is about gaining power for religious and socio-political change, then Jesus was and is a political messiah not only for the people of Israel but for the whole world, including Nigeria. "His whole ministry was political."[22] Jesus was "a model of radical political action."[23] He lifted the curse of sin in human life through his death and resurrection. He established political authority when he said, "All authority has been given to Me in heaven and on earth" (Matt 28:18 NASB). He also gave a political mandate to his followers: "Go therefore and make disciples of all the nations"

---

19. Harper Study Bible, 97.
20. Palma, "Biblical Foundation," 13.
21. Stott, *Issues Facing Christians Today*, 11.
22. Stott, "Human Rights and Human Wrongs," 27.
23. Yoder, *Politics of Jesus*, 2.

(Matt 28:19). Jesus laid the foundation of a new political system: God-centered politics. Stott describes Jesus's politics thus:

> The kingdom of God he proclaimed and inaugurated was a radically new and different social organization, whose values and standards challenged those of the old and fallen community. In this way his teaching had "political" implications. It offered an alternative to the status quo. His kingship, moreover, was perceived as a challenge to Caesar's and he was therefore accused of sedition.[24]

New Political Covenant – the Church

In the Acts of the Apostles we see the establishment of a new political covenant with "the church." In Acts 1:8, Jesus assures the disciples that they would receive "power" when the Holy Spirit came upon them, and then be able to witness for him both in Jerusalem, Judea, Samaria, and to the whole world. In the day of Pentecost, the Holy Spirit came and empowered Christ's followers for religious and political mission, the rule or reign of God among humankind.

The inauguration of the church can be termed as a "political party of Jesus," which ushered in the kingdom of God and the rule of God, in the whole world, including Nigeria. The church is to make disciples of all nations, and not exhibit the individualistic methodology shown by the Christian missionaries over the ages. The children of God cannot make disciples of all nations without political action. From a biblical understanding, politics is a religious tool, a mandated, legitimate responsibility of God's people, the new Israel, the church. Christians belong to "Jesus's Political Party (JPP)" that will bring moral integrity in any society in which they find themselves.

In a nutshell, politics is a human activity ordained by God and "firmly rooted in the biblical tradition. Redemption for the Hebrews had a specifically political meaning in that God had delivered them from the bondage of slavery in Egypt. The Sinai experience marked the formation of Israel as a nation in covenantal relationship with the God of their deliverance. National and social identity was directly tied to their obedience to God."[25] His law is the bedrock of socio-political responsibility. The domination of pagan politics, however, gives a uniquely political character to the New Testament itself. Pharisees, Zealots,

---

24. Stott, *Issues Facing Christians Today*, 13.
25. Simmons, "Morality: Church and Government," 131.

and Sadducees alike formed their social lives largely around the question of the relation of religion to politics. Jesus's mission and ministry are shaped to a large extent by the political options opened to him. "Christ's approach toward politics is determined by their perception of his relationship to God and Caesar. Thus, the early church struggled with a perplexing question: What belongs to Caesar and what belongs to God (Mark 12:13–17)?"[26] This question is still a problem for modern-day Christianity in Nigeria. This is because many see politics in Nigeria only as a "process of controlling the authority to distribute the values of society as supreme arbiter; and the process and institutions for seeing who gets what, how, and when from the resources and assets of Nigeria."[27]

This study on moral integrity is an attempt to unravel the problem of "God and Caesar" in Nigerian politics. "Caesar" is created and ordained by God in any society. What God demands from "Caesar" and his cohorts is integrity. Israel failed as a nation because they lacked moral integrity in the sight of God and wanted to be like other nations. Jesus came to inaugurate a new "Israel" to model or propel moral integrity. How this can be implemented in the politics of Nigeria is our concern.

Integrity in Politics

Integrity comes from the Latin word "integer," which means whole or entire. "A person is said to have integrity if he or she is a complete and definite self and has powers to resist 'disintegration' in the face of temptation, suffering, peer pressure, and other adverse moral influences."[28] Thus, *integrity* as a moral virtue is *the ability to be and to be able to remain a moral entity*, that is, a man or woman in the fullest and deepest sense. It is the quality of being honest and firm in moral principles.[29] Honesty is a basic value of life in which thought, word, and deed fit together into a wholesome existence. When we say a person has integrity in politics, it means the person is selfless, honest, truthful, just, courageous, and compassionate in his or her political involvement. An honest politician is the one who is able to resist political temptation without moral stain. "Lack of integrity is a fault line in the character that jeopardizes all other values and undermines all relationships."[30] In other words, integrity touches

---

26. Simmons, 131.
27. Otite and Ogionwo, *Introduction to Sociological Studies*, 5.
28. Roberts, "Character," 65.
29. BBC English Dictionary, 606.
30. McQuilkin, *Introduction to Biblical Ethics*, 381.

every aspect of human behavior. Therefore, personal integrity in any political system demands honesty and complete freedom from any form of cheating, stealing, corruption, or taking advantage of others.

There is a need to examine the meaning of integrity for a proper understanding in its application to politics, since integrity is the most important ingredient in the political process. It is a human quality most necessary to political stability and accountability. If we are to play a constructive role in the political dialogue of our time, there is a need to understand the concept of integrity and to develop a religious ethic which will be applicable to the current political concerns in Nigeria. Webster's dictionary defines integrity as the "quality or state of being of sound moral principle, uprightness, honesty and sincerity." Webster also defines moral as "relating to, dealing with, or capable of making the distinction between right and wrong in conduct; in accordance with the principles of right and wrong, good or right in the conduct of character . . ."

From an African cultural meaning, integrity as a moral virtue is intrinsically *social*, arising out of the relations between individuals; if there were no such thing as human society, then there would be no such thing as integrity or moral virtue. And because integrity as a moral norm is essentially a social phenomenon – for it can emerge only in a human society in which there is an over-riding concern for harmonious and cooperative living – consideration for the welfare of others and hence, a sense of duty to others, are intrinsic to the meaning and practice of integrity in Nigerian traditional culture.

In the same vein, the Hebrew word for integrity in the Old Testament is *tom*. Apart from "integrity," other words used for *tom* are simplicity, soundness, completeness, uprightness, and perfection. The plural form was one of words on the breastplate of the High Priest, which shows that God obviously holds integrity very highly. The Greek word for integrity (*aletheia*) in the New Testament is often translated as "truth" (Matt 22:16; Mark 12:14). In other words, from the book of Genesis to Revelation, integrity is seen as a valid, desirable character trait. Surely whoever has integrity must be of sound moral principle, honest, and upright in conduct as well as in purity of the heart.[31] Hence there is a three-fold meaning of integrity: (1) unity and wholeness of life, (2) honesty, and (3) purity of heart.

---

31. Murphy and Murphy, *International Minister's Manual*, 65.

Integrity Means Unity and Wholeness of Life

This is to say that integrity as a moral virtue is a dependable and constant loyalty on the part of an individual toward what he or she believes to be right. A man or woman of moral wholeness does not support any actions that are contrary to his or her convictions.[32] In other words, integrity as a wholeness of life means that the individual will be in a right relationship with God, with himself or herself, with his or her fellow humans, as well as the surrounding environment.[33] The Christian concept of integrity gives no aid in violating the demands of conscience. But it does furnish considerable help to the moral person who wants to be loyal to his or her ideals. Politically, it then means that no one can live a well-integrated life unless such person's actions are in harmonious agreement with what he or she honestly believes to be just and right. Hence, the man or woman of integrity will always avoid hypocrisy.[34]

Integrity Means Honesty and Truthfulness

Honesty and integrity involves truthfulness. "Honesty" embraces a family of moral virtues, which might be called the virtues of truthfulness. This includes forthrightness, promising-keeping, intellectual honesty, sincerity, and self-transparency. Forthrightness means the disposition to volunteer truth that one might with some justification have kept to oneself. Intellectual honesty means one's willingness to follow evidence and arguments to the end. Honest integrity implies not only honesty in dealings with other people, but what is often more difficult to achieve, honesty with one's self – that is self-transparency. Thus self-transparency is essential for one's emotions, desires, and preferences, which are basic to self-knowledge and to mature self-hood.[35]

Roberts opines that honesty is manifested in both an emotional response and in behavior – truth-telling which includes rectifying inadvertent deception, and expressing oneself truthfully. A person who is honest rejoices in truth and truth-telling, and such a person is sad and angry in the face of hypocrisy and falsehood. This truthfulness in honest people is rooted in their personalities.[36] In fact, they are lovers of truth. And this love of truth is one of the ways in which a person represents God in his image, that is, to reflect in their character the

---

32. Patterson, *Moral Standards*, 497.
33. McGrath, "Sin and Salvation," 28.
34. Patterson, *Moral Standards*, 497.
35. Patterson, 497; Roberts, "Honesty," 454.
36. Roberts, 454.

intent of God. Those who live and speak the truth demonstrate the character of God and enable trusting relationships to be built up, without which life in society would be difficult. Falsehood, on the other hand, alienates one from God, mars relationships and community, and dehumanizes the one practicing it. Transparent honesty and total trustworthiness, however, are difficult to attain and self-deception is hard to eradicate. "In these areas we need to aim at the highest goals while viewing realistically our own humanness and sinfulness, and humbly accepting God's mercy and grace."[37] A willingness to recognize one's mistakes, weaknesses, and failures, is better than finding excuses or falsifying them – a humble spirit is a pre-requisite to living at one's best.

Integrity Means Purity of the Heart

The concepts as described above are not quite encompassing enough for religious integrity. This is because God also requires that one should be pure in heart. The biblical records extend the meaning of integrity beyond outward conduct to purity of the heart. The psalmist says, "I know, my God, that you test the heart and are pleased with integrity" (1 Chr 29:17). God looks into man's heart and knows that "as he thinks in his heart, so *is* he" (Prov 23:7 NKJV).[38] Thus integrity implies spiritual maturity which is the ability to grow in the character of Christ. The most concise description of Christ's character is the fruit of the spirit. When the Holy Spirit controls our lives, he will produce this kind of fruit in us: love, joy, peace, patience, kindness, goodness, faithfulness, gentleness, and self-control (Gal 5:22–23 NLT). These nine qualities are an expansion of the Great Commandment and a moral expression that portrays a beautiful description of Jesus Christ. Jesus is all the fruit embodied in a single person.[39] To have the fruit of the spirit is to be like Christ, and this should be our mindset even in our political activities.

Purity of the heart is a serious matter because it is the most neglected area in human activities in society. Political corruption or failure, for instance, always starts in the mind, not in circumstances.

> For from within, out of a person's heart, come evil thoughts, sexual immorality, theft, murder, adultery, greed, wickedness, deceit, and

---

37. Hicks, "Truth," 867–868.
38. Murphy and Murphy, *International Minister's Manual*, 65.
39. Warren, *Purpose Driven Life*, 201–202.

eagerness for lustful pleasure, envy, slander, pride, and foolishness. All these vile things come from within. (Mark 7:21–23 NLT)

There is a whole army of evil desires within you. (Jas 4:1 TLB)

Hence integrity demands purity of the heart in any societal activities. It is a spiritual or religious discipline of the thought pattern – the innermost disposition of the heart.

Characteristics of Integrity in Politics

In the above discussion it is obvious that God places greater significance on moral virtue and character than on rules of conduct. The righteous man or woman – the pure in heart – is eternally blessed, and the fruit of the Holy Spirit as disclosed in Galatians 5 are all virtues. Thus, a person who has integrity as an inner virtue does not have divided loyalties – that would be duplicity – nor is he or she merely pretending – that would be hypocrisy. Integrity is a right inner disposition, and a disposition is a tendency to act in certain ways. Disposition is more basic, lasting, and pervasive than the particular motive or intention behind a certain action. It differs from a sudden impulse in being a settled habit of mind, an internalized and often reflective trait. Integrity, like any other virtue, is a character trait that provides inner sanctions on one's particular motives, intentions, and outward conduct.[40]

People with integrity are "whole" people and can be identified by their single-mindedness. Those with integrity have nothing to hide and nothing to fear. Their lives are like open books. A man or woman of integrity is one who has established a system of moral values against which all of life is judged. Integrity is not what people *do* so much as who they *are*. And who such people are, in turn, determines what they do. The moral system of values should be so much a part of a person that one cannot separate integrity from their personality. It becomes the navigating system that guides them. It establishes priorities in their lives and affects what they will accept or reject.[41]

People are all faced with conflicting desires. No one is exempt; even the so-called "spiritual" or "religious" person cannot avoid this battle. Integrity is the factor that determines which desire will prevail. People struggle daily with situations that demand decisions between what one *wants* to do and what one *ought* to do. Moral soundness or integrity establishes the ground rules for

---

40. Holmes, *Ethics*, 116; Maxwell, *Developing the Leader within You*, 36.
41. Maxwell, 36.

resolving these tensions. It determines who a person is and how such a person will respond before the conflict even appears. Thus integrity welds the speaking, thinking, and doing of a man or a woman so that these things are never out of sync. It binds the person together and fosters a spirit of contentment within. This moral virtue will not allow one's lips to violate the heart. When integrity is the referee, there will be consistency; the personal beliefs will be mirrored by the conduct. It allows a person to predetermine what he or she will be irrespective of circumstances, people involved, or the testing ground. Integrity is not the only referee between two desires, urges, or variables – it is the pivotal point between a happy person and a divided spirit. Integrity causes one to be a complete, consistent person no matter what comes their way.[42] Integrity functions as an ethic of *being* that propels human *doing*. In other words, moral integrity is not what a person does as much as whom he or she is. Let's look at some attributes that make integrity so imperative in politics.

Integrity Builds Trusts in Politics

The supreme quality for any successful human activities is unquestionably integrity. Without it, no real success is possible, no matter whether in the public sector or in a private enterprise. If someone's associates find him or her guilty of being false or they discover that such a person lacks forthright integrity, he or she will fail. The person's teachings and actions must square with each other. The imperative need, therefore, is unmistakable integrity and high-quality sound purpose.[43]

The basic idea of trust is a relational quality. Trust is therefore foundational to human growth, development, and activities. Implicit within the idea of trust as a relational concept is the notion of reciprocity, especially from moral perspectives. Speaking about the reciprocity of trust, Bridger writes, "The effective operation of trust between persons requires that both parties be willing to trust each other, since one-sided trust is unstable. A reciprocal relationship is thus created. Out of reciprocity arises moral obligation."[44] That is to say, the soul of trust creates a sense of two-way fairness, which governs human relationships. For the maintenance of such fairness, those involved must recognize that a moral obligation is laid upon them to act according to the fairness criterion.

---

42. Maxwell, 36.
43. Maxwell, 38.
44. Bridger, "Trust," 866.

To be fair means "acceptable and appropriate" action or behavior in political activities; "treating everyone equally and according to the rules or law." Thus fairness is "the quality of treating people equally or in a way that is reasonable" especially in political affairs.[45] The Lord spoke to the Israelites through Moses saying, "Do not pervert justice; do not show partiality to the poor or favoritism to the great, but judge your neighbor fairly" (Lev 19:15). God expects politicians to be fair and loving to everyone, irrespective of position and status. I believe politics is a calling by God especially for those who are Christians. "Being absolutely righteous, God is by nature adamantly opposed to all evil. He will always confront ungodliness in our lives with the intent to make us holy."[46] God, who is righteous in all things, expects righteousness for Nigerian politicians as well as all Nigerians.

In the Bible, trust in politics is built through "covenant." The biblical concept of covenant was similar to the contemporary Near-Eastern political covenants which were agreements between parties involving reciprocal promises and obligations. Such covenants could be between fellow human beings, between God and individuals, or between God and his people. In Israel it is encapsulated in the divine covenant formula, "I will be your God and you will be my people" (Lev 26:12 NLT). Thus integrity is building an impeccable trust, that is, maintaining a faultless relationship in politics.[47]

Integrity Influences Value in Politics

Integrity is the human quality most necessary to human activities – including political activity. Thus it has high influence value on sound moral judgments, which regrettably, we tend to forget in Nigeria. Value is that quality which makes something helpful, useful, or desirable. It is the social principle, goal, or standard held by an individual, class, society, etc., and value judgment is the estimate made of the worth or goodness of a person, action, event, or the like.[48]

There are various distinctions in the use of the word value. In the first place, it functions in a concrete sense when one speaks of concepts such as of "Christian values," or when one differentiates "material values," such as cars or property, from "spiritual values," such as the knowledge of God. When one

---

45. A. S. Hornby, ed. "Fair, Fairness," *Oxford Advanced Learner's Dictionary*, 552–553.
46. Blackaby, ed., *The Blackaby Study Bible*, 159.
47. Bridger, "Trust," 866.
48. *Longman Dictionary of Contemporary English*, s.v. "Value"; Maxwell, *Developing the Leader within You*, 40.

values the knowledge of God over acquiring property, that person has made a comparative "value judgment" to the effect that knowing God is preferable to acquiring property. In the second place, some human values may be moral, others non-moral. The sorts of things that are morally good or bad, Reid writes, "are persons or qualities of persons such as traits of character (virtues and vices), intentions, dispositions, emotions, and motives. On the other hand, things like property, or experiences like knowledge, may be non-morally good or bad. Finally, material possessions like money or property may have only utility value that is value useful for some purpose."[49]

In a biblical ethic, God may properly be thought to have value in each of these concepts, especially where it is understood that only the Godhead has intrinsic value, and that every other thing or person, their properties and relations, have value (moral and non-moral) in relation to him alone. "Christian ethics understands God to be the objective [as objectivists see value], unitary ground of all moral values, and Christ to be the perfect moral exemplar of those values."[50] It is in this sense that integrity has a high influence value especially in politics.

Integrity Facilitates High Standards of Responsibility

Political stalwarts ought to live by higher standards than ordinary persons in society. This insight is exactly opposite of most people's thoughts concerning politics. In the world of perks and privileges that accompanies the climb to success, little attention is given to responsibilities of the upward journey. In politics one can give up anything, except responsibility, either for oneself or ones' organization. "Every right implies a responsibility; every opportunity, an obligation; every possession, a duty." In the political arena, one discovers that too many people are ready to assert their rights but not to assume their responsibilities.[51] The Scripture says, "From everyone who has been given much, much will be required" (Luke 12:48).

Responsibility requires a high standard of character. It is a complex concept involving motions of *accountability* and *obligation*. Accountability looks back to some deed done or attitude held. Obligation looks forward to moral demands that need to be met in relationship. Responsibility fosters relationships, deeds, and attitudes, which may attract either commendation or condemnation.

---

49. Reid, "Values, Value Judgments," 872.
50. Reid, 873.
51. Maxwell, *Developing the Leader within You*, 40–41.

From a Christian perspective, moral responsibility in terms of accountability and obligation involves responsibility to God in worship, responsibility to our fellow human being in just dealings, responsibility to oneself in keeping a clear conscience, and responsibility to the environment in being a wise steward of the good earth, which is an obligation to God rather than to nature itself. In other words, from a biblical perspective, responsibilities to others, to self, and to nature are subjects of responsibility to God (cf. Gen 1–11). The significance of the concept of responsibility which integrity facilitates is manifold. God is the judge of every human action and activity. All humankind stands in relationship to him. Relationship brings responsibility and with responsibility comes accountability and obligation.[52]

Integrity Means "Being before Doing"

This is a crucial dimension of integrity for it involves the move from the focus on *doing* to a concern for *being*.[53] It is personal character formation. When attention is given to "character" the reference is to moral elements we often consider internal, such as motives, dispositions, attitudes, intentions, and perceptions. These belong to moral *being* as aspects of our moral identity. In other words, it expresses character, individually or collectively. These traits reflect who we are morally. That is, moral virtue pertains to qualities of sound moral character, which will also reflect the social arrangements that make for a society of sound moral character. Thus the *being* nature of integrity nurtures courageous and compassionate people, honest and just ones. It fosters an ethos of fair and equal treatment of all social groups.[54] In fact, integrity is an ethic of being.

The *being* ought to be the foundation of the ethic of *doing* in politics. The doing refers not to interior qualities of character but to decisions and actions themselves. A normative ethic of doing is the primary focus of many ethicists. They understand ethics primarily as the attempt to develop standards of conduct. Thus they argue that ethics or morality is concerned above all with determining what one should *do*. Consequently they propose what one might call an "ethic of doing."[55] It determines the rightness and wrongness of acts, but more importantly is the normative ethic of being which fosters integrity.

---

52. Cole, "Responsibility," 734–736.
53. Grenz, *Moral Quest*, 207–208.
54. Birch and Rasmussen, *Bible and Ethics in the Christian Life*, 40–41.
55. Grenz, *Moral Quest*, 27.

Instead, Nigerians should promote an ethic of *being* over only the *doing* ethic in political activities. We must live godly lives and apply godliness in everything we do in politics. It is not merely "head knowledge," but the godly wisdom of being righteous while doing what is righteous in every political situation. However, this wisdom is not an inherent human ability but the gift of God. James 1:5 says, "If any of you lacks wisdom, let him ask of God, who gives to all liberally and without reproach, and it will be given to him" (NKJV). God knows what is within our hearts; we do not. God will at times allow politicians or anyone to undergo trials and temptations as a way of bringing to surface those things in our lives that are impure or ungodly. When we repent of our sin and learn from our failures, we grow into maturity in politics.[56]

Integrity Is a Hard-Won Achievement

Integrity is not a given factor in people's lives. "It is a result of self-discipline, inner trust, and a decision to be relentlessly honest in all situations in our lives."[57] Unfortunately, strength of character is not common among politicians. As a result, there are few contemporary models of integrity. Nigerian culture has produced a few enduring heroes, models of virtue, such as Balewa, Azikiwe, Awolowo, Bello, Macaulay and others. We have become a nation of imitators, with only a few leaders worth imitating.

The meaning of integrity has also been eroded. In the modern world, the word *integrity* conjures up ideas of prudishness or narrow-mindedness. In the world of intellectuals, when the meanings of words are manipulated, foundational values such as integrity can be pulverized overnight. Integrity has become antithetic to national growth. The overarching philosophy of life that guides Nigerian culture revolves around a materialistic, consumer mentality. The craving need of the moment supersedes consideration of values that have eternal significance. "Integrity is the glue that holds our way of life together. We must constantly strive to keep our integrity intact. When wealth is lost, nothing is lost; when health is lost, something is lost; when character is lost, all is lost."[58] Thus, integrity is a hard-won achievement, a virtue that needs to be cultivated and held in high esteem by all Nigerians.

Integrity is a hard-won achievement that needs to be commended. For example, Justice Ephraim O. Akpata's personal integrity, professional

---

56. Grenz, 45.
57. Grenz, 45.
58. Grenz, 45.

competence, management skill, organizational techniques, and patriotism stood out clearly, and as the Independent National Electoral Commission (INEC) chairman he was sincerely commended publicly by Nigerians and foreign nationals in the election that brought in Obasanjo as the president. He brought hope that democracy could flourish in Nigerian politics, in spite of the past political failures.

Integrity Is a Priceless and Godly Treasure

Integrity in biblical Christianity is a priceless treasure. This is doubly so for Christian politicians. Great and powerful biblical characters walked in godly integrity. God always ultimately blesses his men and women of integrity.[59] The entire Scripture, both Old Testament and New Testament, see integrity as a desirable character trait. The divine imperative is that one who has integrity must be of sound moral principle, be honest, and be upright in conduct.[60] As said in the previous section, God, through the pages of the Bible, extends the definition of integrity beyond conduct to purity of the heart.

Seen from the perspective of the whole, the biblical viewpoint does not lead to a concern mainly for acts in themselves and hence for a pure ethic of doing. In addition to an obvious interest in right actions, the biblical writers show a great concern for what motivates conduct. The wisdom literature of the Bible suggests that integrity leads to a good reputation, and indeed consistent, authentic, courageous people do become known as persons of integrity. The book of Proverbs points out the exceedingly great value of such a reputation: "A good name is more desirable than great riches; to be esteemed is better than silver or gold" (Prov 22:1). "Then you will win favor and a good name in the sight of God and man" (Prov 3:4). Unfortunately, most Nigerians in politics prefer great riches to a good name; thus, they become known for their moral misconducts and for international money laundering. The significant role of motivation likewise formed a central aspect of Jesus's critique of the religious leaders of his day. Outwardly they evidenced conformity to the Old Testament law, but Jesus observed that their motives were wrong. These people were only seeking their own benefit; they were motivated by selfishness.[61]

Even the quest for right motives does not tap into the central heartbeat of the New Testament conception of the moral life. Motivation is itself related

---

59. Murphy and Murphy, *International Minister's Manual*, 63.
60. Murphy and Murphy, 65.
61. Grenz, *Moral Quest*, 229.

to something deeper. For the New Testament authors, the ultimate wellspring of action is our "heart" or "affections." "Jesus himself declared that God's intention for humankind does not stop with mere outward conformity to laws, especially humanly devised legal structures. A focus on outward obedience fails to acknowledge that the human 'heart' is the source of evil actions (Mark 7:14–23; Matt 12:33–37)."[62] According to Jesus, these people honored God with their lips, but their hearts were far from his heavenly Father (Matt 15:8). Thus, integrity is a heart treasure.

Jesus's "focus on the heart as the wellspring of action led [him] – again following the Old Testament itself – to conclude that the greatest commandments were to love God and neighbor (Matt 22:37–40). In so doing, he reunited the inward and the outward. For Jesus, love meant an inward affection turned toward God and others, as well as the outward action such a godly affection produces. This uniting of the inward and the outward, which characterized Jesus's ethical teaching, leads Christians to the concept of integrity. It suggests that a focus on integrity, and thus on character or virtue, must be central to our statement of the Christian ethic."[63] In this direction, modern thinkers like Alasdair Macintyre see the ethical life as involving "singleness of purpose" or the virtue of integrity.[64] Indeed, it is a priceless treasure.

Integrity Fosters Divine-Human Relationship

Integrity "lies in the God who is faithful to the divine covenant despite human failure and sin."[65] In setting forth an ethic of integrity, Christians can appeal to the ways of the God of the biblical story for the foundation of understanding moral virtues such as faithfulness and justice. Even integrity itself can only be defined in connection with God's own character as depicted in the biblical narrative of the divine covenant-keeper. We can also appeal to the example of the biblical God for another function as well. God's way in the universe forms a model for us to live morally in the world. "For the Christian, integrity ultimately involves living in such a way that one's life mirrors God's own nature and thereby depicts what God is like. In this task, Christians appeal above all

---

62. Grenz, 229.
63. Grenz, 229.
64. Grenz, 229.
65. Grenz, 231.

to the life of Jesus the Christ, who is Immanuel, "God with us" (Matt 1:23) and the incarnate word of God (John 1:14).[66]

The biblical foundation for the life of integrity is embedded in Christ Jesus. The New Testament writers, especially Paul, show the essence of the Christian life as a union with Christ, or Christ in us, which constitutes our person (e.g. Col 1:27). In other words, Christians gain their foundational identity from the biblical narrative of Jesus. One ought to be sincerely devoted to Christ and to the heavenly Father who loved and saved him. Thus, in all of life, Christians should want to be conformed to the "image of Christ" both in the inward being and in the outward conduct (2 Cor 3:18). The New Testament on this basis also set forth a special concept of spiritual integrity. The Christian moral life is "walking in the spirit" (Gal 5:16), that is, being imbued with the same spirit who guided our Lord Jesus himself. This indwelling Holy Spirit, the spirit of Christ, forms a Christ-like character within the disciple and thereby becomes the author of the life of integrity. Thus, for the biblical Christianity the life of integrity is more than merely "Jesus and I for each tomorrow."[67] It is living according to the ideals of Jesus Christ that embody and transmit Christ's vision. For this reason biblical integrity cannot be lived in an isolated, purely personal ethic. Rather the life of integrity, from the biblical viewpoint, begins as the Christian develops an awareness of personal identity within the context of the fellowship of the body of Christ.

In the same vein, the biblical concept of integrity means living out a sense of foundational status (who I am as a child of God) and a sense of calling or vocation (who I am in the program of God). "But even this identity cannot be isolated from that of the group. Each Christian participates in a particular people. And even when living, for example, 'in the world of politics,' each person carries a personal responsibility as a representative of that people, the community of faith."[68] In this way, integrity fosters the divine-human relationship.

Biblical Characters of Integrity

There are great personalities in the Bible that walked in godly integrity. God ultimately blesses great people that exhibit integrity. These men and women attracted God's favor as a result of the integrity shown in their daily lives.

---

66. Grenz, 231.
67. Grenz, 233.
68. Grenz, 233.

Noah

Noah's integrity brought him a gracious invitation into the safety of the Ark among his contemporaries. Noah was a "righteous man" (Gen 6:9) having the righteousness that comes from faith (Heb 11:7), and had close communion with his Creator, as indicated by the expression he "walked with God" (Gen 6:9). He is also described as a man without fault among the people of his time, who had all sunk to a very low moral level. It was a situation that God lamented:

> The LORD saw how great the wickedness of the human race had become on the earth, and that every inclination of the thoughts of the human heart was only evil all the time. The LORD regretted that he had made human beings on the earth, and his heart was deeply troubled. (Gen 6:5–6)

This is one of the Bible's most vivid descriptions of total moral depravity. And because the nature of humans remain unchanged, things are no better after the flood (Gen 8:21).[69]

God's gracious call to Noah to come into the ark is a very honorable testament to his integrity. Noah's distinguished moral integrity shows that those who are righteous before God, the One who searches hearts, he cannot be deceived by other people's character. God takes notice of those who are morally sound and righteous; he is pleased with them. God is a witness to, and will be a witness for, his people's moral integrity. God's reaction to Noah's integrity also shows that in a special way, he is pleased with those that are morally good in bad times and places. "Those who keep themselves pure in times of common iniquity God will keep safe in times of common calamity."[70] Indeed, Noah found favor in the sight of God because of his integrity. His integrity preserved him and his family and this depicts how important integrity is in God's sight.

Joseph

Joseph is another character in the Bible who was very aware of, and concerned with, personal integrity. He was the eleventh and favorite son of Jacob, and he was Rachel's first-born. His life story of stout integrity is told in Genesis 37–50, with commentary in Psalms 105:17–22, Acts 7:9–16, and Hebrews 11:22.[71] These stories describe Joseph as cheerful and uncomplaining, and possessed

---

69. Mitchell, "Noah," 838.
70. Henry, *Matthew Henry's Commentary*, 18.
71. Goddard, "Joseph," 299.

with an ambition that no adversity could destroy. There are many sudden and striking contrasts in Joseph's life. These include Joseph's change from a petted and spoiled boy to a slave in Egypt; from an overseer of his master's house to a prisoner in a dungeon; and from that dungeon to the governorship of the most powerful empire of the age. Joseph wins all his successes because of his moral values to his fellow men and women. He is never promoted by means of any miracle or conquests of power, but by sound moral integrity, faithfulness, business sagacity, and loyal service to others. He is truly a hero of human service.[72]

Having been sold by the Ishmaelites to Potipher, the captain of Pharaoh's guard, "Joseph took his position as a slave. But he was so faithful and honest in all his duties, and worked with such success for the interest of his master, that he soon won the complete trust of the Egyptian and was made overseer of everything belonging to his household."[73] In spite of the fact that Joseph was far from home in the midst of the lax moral life of Egypt, he refused to participate in lustful wickedness, for he had a strong moral code and a fear of God. His response to Potiphar's wife's seduction was:

> "With me in charge," he told her, "my master does not concern himself with anything in the house; everything he owns he has entrusted to my care. No one is greater in his house than I am. My master has withheld nothing from me except you, because you are his wife. How then could I do such a wicked thing and sin against God." (Gen 39:8–9)

When the tempter persisted, he lost his garment, but he refused to lose his innocence and fled from the scene of temptation (39:12). He is then unjustly thrown into prison, his only crime being his attractiveness and moral integrity.

But Joseph's persistent integrity exemplified the spiritual power of divine grace operating in the life of a person who takes a stand to walk with God. His demonstration of unusual moral integrity elevated him from chief trustee in his prison to prime minister in the then-known world empire to save the world from a great famine.[74] Joseph's moral integrity in the midst of misfortunes shows that integrity pays at the end. Unjust adversity cannot destroy a man or a woman of faith and integrity, if such a person will manifest a cheerful and helpful spirit. God overrules evil for good, so that all things can work together for good for the one who stands on moral integrity.

---

72. Tidwell, *The Bible, Period by Period*, 73–78.
73. Tidwell, 74.
74. Tullock, *Old Testament Story*, 54.

Uriah

Uriah the Hittite demonstrates his integrity as a soldier. Uriah was a mighty and loyal soldier in David's army (2 Sam 11). While Uriah was away fighting for Israel, David seduced his wife, Bathsheba. The aftermath of this defilement was pregnancy for Bathsheba and a moral indictment to David (11:2–5). What followed is a vivid example of how a deeply religious man can be so concerned with protecting his reputation that he can forget his religious principles. David tried by various means to make it possible that Bathsheba's husband, Uriah, would believe he was the father-to-be. But Uriah, being a loyal soldier in David's army, would not cooperate.[75]

Uriah demonstrated his patriotic integrity before the adulterous king. When David asked him why he refused even to enter his home, he responded:

> "The ark and Israel and Judah, are staying in temporary shelters, and my lord Joab and the servants of my lord are camping in the open field. Shall I then go to my house to eat and to drink and to lie with my wife? By your life and the life of your soul, I will not do this thing." (2 Sam 11:11)

As a man of integrity, he felt it was unpatriotic to enjoy the pleasure of wife and home while his friends were fighting. Finally, in desperation, David sent Uriah back to the battle with a secret order to Joab to put him in the front lines so he would be killed (11:6–21).[76] Thus, Uriah did not survive the war, for he died in active service.

What great moral and patriotic integrity Uriah had! He was absolutely unyielding doing what he knew to be right. And Uriah's integrity is demonstrated in vivid contrast with David's obvious lack of integrity in this instance. No Nigerian soldier, especially, can read this account and not have great admiration for "General Uriah" and his incredible integrity. This biblical account demonstrates how important integrity is for God's leaders.

Job

Job is another man whose lifestyle attracted God's favor. Job's account begins with his great piety in general and his great prosperity in particular. Indeed he was a man of great wealth and high social position, which attracted the malice of Satan against him and the permission to try his constancy (Job

---

75. Murphy and Murphy, *International Minister's Manual*, 63.
76. Tullock, *Old Testament Story*, 141.

1:6–12). As a result of divine permission, Satan robbed him of his wealth, his ten children, and finally his health. His relations and fellow townsmen interpreted his misfortunes as a divine punishment for gross sin and threw him out of the town, the rabble taking a particular pleasure in this. His wife accepted the common opinion and urged him to expedite the inevitable end by cursing God.[77] She said, "Are you still maintaining your integrity? Curse God and die!" (Job 2:9).

Job was visited by three friends, Eliphaz, Bildad and Zophar, also members of the rich and affluent as he had been. When they saw his plight they shared popular opinion and could only sit in silence with Job on the dunghill outside the city gate for seven days of mourning for a man as good as dead.[78] Job chided his friends,

> "But now be so kind as to look at me.
>   Would I lie to your face?
> Relent, do not be unjust;
>   reconsider, for my integrity is at stake.
> Is there any wickedness on my lips?
>   Can my mouth not discern malice?" (Job 6:28–30)

"The Bible tells us that Job was a person of strong character and unparalleled godliness."[79] His character appears in a remarkable light as "blameless and upright" (Job 1:8). Blameless "does not imply sinless perfection, which is never claimed for Job. Rather it encourages one to think of Job as a moral all-rounder, a man of balanced, full-orbed character."[80] He was a man of virtue and integrity – a man who believed in God and obeyed him in a way that is exemplary to every Nigerian.[81]

Daniel

Daniel is another distinguished biblical character who exhibited sound integrity in the political arena in a foreign land. He was a man of extraordinary wisdom and righteousness whose name is coupled with Noah and Job (Ezek 14:14, 20) and who is mentioned again in Ezekiel 28:3. Daniel's wisdom and integrity

---

77. Ellison, "Job," 598.
78. Ellison, 598.
79. Heavenor, "Job," 423.
80. Heavenor, 423.
81. Egner, *Knowing God through Job*, 11.

had become proverbial as early as 603 BC (Dan 2:1), a number of years before Ezekiel spoke of it. Daniel was an Israelite of royal or noble descent, and was carried away captive to Babylon by King Nebuchadnezzar in the third year of Jehoiakim, with various companions trained for the king's service (Dan 1:1–6).[82] He carried along his religious integrity with him into exile.

Daniel gained a reputation first as an interpreter of other men's visions (chs. 2–5), then of his own, in which he predicted the future triumph of the Messianic kingdom (chs. 7–12). Renowned for sagacity and political integrity, he successfully occupied leading governmental posts under Nebuchadnezzar, Belshazzar, Cyrus and Darius. His sound, moral principles in governance attracted jealousy among the ruling class of his time. He was an honest and faithful administrator. Chapter 6 of the book of Daniel gives a vivid picture of his administrative integrity. Verses 3–5 say:

> Now Daniel so distinguished himself among the administrators and the satraps by his exceptional qualities that the king planned to set him over the whole kingdom. At this, the administrators and the satraps tried to find grounds for charges against Daniel in his conduct of government affairs, but they were unable to do so. They could find no corruption in him, because he was trustworthy and neither corrupt nor negligent. Finally these men said, "We will never find any basis for charges against this man Daniel unless it has something to do with the Law of his God." (Dan 6:3–5)

What an incredible moral life! Even Daniel's political counterparts could not find a drop of accusation against him. So his conspirators had to lie, stating that all the royal administrators supported the proposed decree. They knew that Daniel, totally unaware of the proposal, was the foremost of the three administrators (cf. Dan 6:7). This however, did not shake Daniel's religious integrity. Their plan to discredit Daniel before the king did not affect Darius's trust in Daniel. Rather, the king prayed for him (Dan 6:16). His integrity attracted divine rescue and victory over his enemies. Daniel's moral and religious integrity heralds God's sovereignty among the heathen: "The Most High God is sovereign over all kingdoms on earth" (Dan 5:21). What a great challenge to the contemporary political stalwarts!

---

82. Douglas and Whitcomb, "Daniel," 262.

Zechariah and Elizabeth

In the New Testament, Luke, while speaking of Zechariah and Elizabeth (the soon to be the parents of John the Baptist), wrote, "Both of them were righteous in the sight of God, observing all the Lord's commands and decrees blamelessly" (Luke 1:6). They were a religious couple and were faithful to the Lord. Not that they never did anything that fell short of their duties, but it was their consistency that counted. Though they were not sinless, yet they were blameless; nobody could charge them with any open scandalous sin; they lived honestly and inoffensively.

Simeon, Joseph, and Jesus

There are other characters in the New Testament given similar praise, such as Simeon, who was given special insight by the Spirit so that he would recognize the Christ (Luke 2:25). Also Joseph, the father of Jesus, who was zealous in keeping the law, was commended (see Matt 1:19).[83] And even those who were against our Lord Jesus Christ commended him as a man of integrity. "Teacher" they said, "we know you are a man of integrity and that you teach the way of God in accordance with the truth. You aren't swayed by others" (Matt 22:16).

This study will use Jesus as a model of integrity in Nigerian politics.

Conclusion

The study of the concept of integrity so far shows that integrity is a priceless treasure. Men and women of integrity are honored. From a biblical perspective, God also esteems integrity. Note David's prayer, "I know, my God, that you test the heart and are pleased with integrity" (1 Chr 29:17). Since integrity is so precious to God, we will carefully examine its place, or lack thereof, in Nigerian politics. Both in the Old Testament and New Testament we see moral integrity as a valid, desirable character trait. From God's perspective, the person of integrity must be of sound moral principle, honest, and upright in conduct, and it is more of our *being* than our *doing*. This seems to be the major challenge in the Nigerian political process. However, in the next chapter we will begin with a review of some related works as regard to politics in relation to ethics and religion.

---

83. Murphy and Murphy, *International Minister's Manual*, 64.

2

Politics in Relation to Ethics and Religion

The coming of Christianity and Islam marked a revolution of ethical conduct in Nigerian politics. It introduced a religious conception of "good" into Nigerian thought. Islam will be discussed a bit later, but in the Christian view, for instance, a person is totally dependent upon God and cannot achieve goodness in practical politics by means of their will or intelligence, or by any underhanded means. It can only be achieved with the help of God's grace in Christ Jesus. The primary Christian ethical belief which is ideal in Nigerian politics is stated in the golden rule: "Treat people the same way you want them to treat you" (Matt 7:12). It is also seen in the injunctions to love one's neighbor as oneself (see Lev 19:18), to love one's "political enemies" (see Matt 5:44), and in Jesus's saying, "Render to Caesar the things that are Caesar's, and to God the things that are God's" (Matt 22:21).

There are numerous materials written on politics in relation to ethics and religion but only the few that are related to the objective of this study will be reviewed. There are also difficulties in getting sources that treat integrity in relation to politics. Most of the material under review focuses attention on the apolitical attitude of most Nigerians. The feeling of most Nigerians, both literate and illiterate, about politics, is pessimism. Politics is conceived as a governmental activity that has to do with stealing, lying, cheating, getting rich quick, and other dubious activities during the process of elections or while in power.[1] Thus, political stalwarts are perceived as dishonest people. Indeed, the actions of most politicians confirm this sweeping generalization.

---

1. Yamsat, *Role of the Church in Democratic Governance*, 1–9.

Nigerians' conception of what politics means to them is expressed in metaphors. Some see politics as "food," while some others perceive it as "war." A politician once said, "Politics is my life, it is in my own blood." In other words, politics is the very life of such a person; he requires it to survive. In this sense, a politician can be politically "dead" or such a person can commit "political suicide." With such a concept of politics in terms of life, politics is overestimated and it is sought for at the expense of life and property.

However, patriotic Nigerians see politics as a "game." As a game, there are rules that guide its players so as to prevent moral lawlessness and injuries. In a game, there is always a winner and a loser, a victory and a defeat. Each of them is acceptable to good players. An unwillingness to accept defeat leads to intolerance and aggression. Thus, the noble aspects of a political game includes such moral values as cooperation, fairness, joy in taking part, a sharpening of the intellect, and justice in seeing that the best person wins. Such were the attitudes of the Nigerian heroes of the past, people like Macaulay, Ikoku, Akintola, Okpara, Balewa, Bello, Azikiwe, Awolowo, Tarka, Ironsi, Murtala, Aminu Kano, and others. These patriots believed that Nigeria was one indivisible and indissoluble sovereign state to be known by the name of the Federal Republic of Nigeria.

As a result of some ugly phenomena in Nigerian politics, the majority of Christians shy away from politics. Most of them joined the bandwagon of seeing the dichotomies between church and state, spiritual and material, and religious and secular, which were created by eighteenth- and nineteenth-century Western Christianity, as a political reaction to the excesses and oppression by the established order in the Western world. However, politics has to do with happiness and the good of people of any given society. Yamsat rightly said, "It has to do with the fair sharing of power and the wealth of the nation to the rightful citizens."[2] It is against this background that most authors reviewed here write to support the fact that religion has a vital role to play in politics in the understanding of morality and ethical principles. Religion cannot be divorced from politics. It is religion that propels morality in political actions and reactions.

First, therefore, we need to define *religion*. Emile Durkheim defined religion as "a unified system of beliefs and practices relative to sacred things, that is, things set apart and forbidden – beliefs and practices which unite into one single moral community called a Church, and all those who adhere to

---

2. Yamsat, 9.

them."[3] Thus, to be religious is to have our attention fixed on God and our fellow human beings in relation to God. "Pure and undefiled religion before God and the Father is this: to visit orphans and widows in their trouble, *and to keep oneself unspotted from the world*" (Jas 1:27 NKJV). "Religion is to do right. It is to love, it is to serve, it is to think, and it is to be humble," according to Ralph W. Emerson. John, the beloved disciple, sees religion itself as nothing else but love to God and mankind. "Whoever lives in love lives in God" (1 John 4:16). If the religious concept of love were to be applied to politics, Nigerian democracy would blossom.

In this study the word "religion" will be used to mean the service and worship of the Almighty God in Nigeria. Nigeria is a heterogenic society with many religions and tribes. Religion is an important phenomenon in contemporary Nigeria as it affects every segment of Nigerian society. Christianity, Islam and African Traditional Religion are the most widely practiced religions in Nigeria, all claiming belief in God the Creator. Religion is a faith-based process that is capable of impacting governance and the behavioral attitudes of every Nigerian. Although Nigeria is a secular state, "she has to her credit a written Constitution being operated for the effective democratic governance of her population, comprising peoples of different religious freedom and cultural backgrounds."[4] However, some politicians have manipulated religious freedom for their selfish interests.

On the grounds of fundamental rights and freedom of religion, for instance, Islamic communities demand a full implementation of the Islamic law known as Shar'ia. In Kano and Zamfara, two men had their hands amputated – one in each of the states – as a punishment for stealing a goat and a cow respectively. Here, religion willfully handicapped able-bodied men where it should be improving the poor conditions of disabled persons.

In another example, an unmarried woman, Safiya Hussaini, was charged by Gwadabawa *Shar'ia* court in Sokoto for adultery and she was convicted and sentenced to death by stoning according to Islamic law. A similar situation happened in Katsina State where Aminat Lawal was accused of committing adultery. She too was charged by the court and sentenced to death by stoning. On both occasions, Hajiya Aisha Ishmail, the Minister of Women Affairs, played an important role in coordinating information and legal representation for the

---

3. Durkheim, *Elementary Form of the Religious Life*, online.

4. Yesufu, "The Impact of Religion," http://www.scielo.org.za/scielo.php?script=sci_arttext&pid=S1017-04992016000100003. For more definitions of religion, see ReligionFacts.com, www.religionfacts.com/religion.

accused women. Each case went to an appeal court where the convictions were overturned, so both women were discharged and acquitted. Just as an adulterous woman was rescued by Jesus from being stoned to death in the name of religion (John 8:3–11), so Hajiya Aisha Ishmail saved Safiya and Aminat from the death penalty imposed by Shar'ia courts.

Politics and Ethics

This book considers Christian political ethics; therefore, it is paramount that it helps us to see the dire need of integrity in politics, which is our focus. The close relationship between ethics and the problem of governance has been recognized since the days of the early Greek philosophers. Plato, for instance, in his book, *The Republic*, makes the study of ethics an essential part of the training of his philosopher-kings. According to Patterson, Plato could not do otherwise without changing his whole conception of human nature and society. To him, the good governance of any nation is like the good individual functioning harmoniously toward the welfare of the society. In other words, until the political leaders and politicians have this concept clearly in mind, they can neither make nor enforce those moral laws which are necessary for good governance.[5]

Aristotle, the Greek philosopher who created and named ethics as a discipline,[6] recognized the importance of the study of ethics for dealing intelligently with matters pertaining to the state. In his *Nicomachean Ethics*, he argues that the art that treats ethics is politics. He buttresses this point further in that ethics requires politics as the venue of its implementation and that ethics in a fundamental sense is politics. "Ethics increasingly expresses itself for us as direct, participatory politics."[7] Patterson writes, "Since governments exist for the sake of promoting the good life, those who have to do with affairs of state should have a clear understanding of what it is that they are trying to promote."[8]

Utilitarians believe that the aim of government is the provision of "the greatest happiness of the greatest number." In pursuing this aim, the government needs to establish many devices in order to produce happiness in such a way as to diffuse it as widely as possible across the society. The characteristics of a democratic society, according to utilitarianism, are: equality, respect for a

---

5. Strang, "Ethics as Politics," 274.
6. Dzurgba, *Principles of Ethics*, 1.
7. Patterson, *Moral Standards*, 432.
8. Patterson, 432.

human life, the liberty of the individual, the sovereignty of the people, and the rule of law. Thus, Utilitarians recognize the importance of moral values in politics and governance. The great scholars of the utilitarian school in its most flourishing period (the beginning of the nineteenth century) were Jeremy Bentham, James Mill, and his son, John Stuart Mill. These Utilitarians were themselves social reformers who worked for the betterment of humankind. Though Utilitarians valued morality, they regarded utility as the one and only moral principle that underlies all human acts and social policies.[9]

In his book, *Nigerian Politics and Moral Behaviour*, Dzurgba sees the urgent need for ethics to be incorporated into Nigerian politics. Speaking from a Nigerian context he said that electorates and politicians need knowledge of ethics for an immediate use. Political stalwarts need ethics for practising politics. An elector or a politician is born with ethical qualities in his personality.[10] The author argues that everyone has capacities for knowledge, reasoning, judgement, opinions, choices, rejection, and freedom. These natural abilities enable politicians and non-politicians to initiate, plan, execute, postpone, prevent, or avoid an action. In other words, a politician or an elector has a freedom of action. He or she does not act under compulsion or duress. This means one is not compelled, forced, or coerced to act. When these capacities are functioning normally, one is able to ask and answer moral questions. Is the candidate an honest person? Is he or she competent? It is in this sense, Dzurgba says, that an elector or a politician is an ethical person.[11]

Moral Values in Politics

The above reviews have established the fact that ethics is related to politics. In this assertion of ethics as politics, we need also to answer a fundamental question. Is there any need for moral values in doing politics? Again, Dzurgba says, moral values permeate and medicate meaningful interactions and relationship in politics. "Values mediate meaningful integration and adaptation in a political system." They "order relationships, interactions, integration and adaptation."[12] According to Dzurgba, in politics, the state has a sovereign authority with which it employs a physical compulsion, a physical force. It has a power to coerce, that is, a power to command. The state has a superior

---

9. Dzurgba, *Principles of Ethics*, 42–44.
10. Dzurgba, *Nigerian Politics and Moral Behaviour*, 19.
11. Dzurgba, 18.
12. Dzurgba, 41.

force and it is the final arbiter of the state's power to command obedience to its authority. But the physical force of the state is not the ultimate basis of the citizens' allegiance to the sovereign authority of the state.[13]

Dzurgba stresses further that the citizens of any given state may be subjected to and led by coercive measures, but in the final analysis, allegiance cannot be achieved and maintained by means of coercion. Thus, he argues that the need arises for constraints without physical force and appeals without coercion, as the ultimate basis in gaining the citizens' patriotic allegiance to the nation. Dzurgba asserts that such constraints and appeals are moral constraints and appeals.[14]

> Moral values permeate the individual's conscience and the collective conscience of all the citizens. Environmental and constitutional frames of reference are meaningless unless there are moral standards for evaluation of behaviour or conduct. These moral standards or principles determine what is legitimate and permissible as well as what is anomalous or irregular and is proscribed or denounced as dangerous.[15]

This means that it is the conviction of the citizens that there is a healthy balance between duty and reward, responsibility and benefits, freedom and constraint, that determines their loyalty to the political system.

Moral values help to determine indispensable behavior patterns. They are part and parcel of people's lives because they serve the basic needs and provide the basis upon which people organize their social lives, in particular, and their existence, in general. Politically, therefore, the individual understands and appreciates the significance of patriotism, faithfulness, loyalty, honesty, fairness, and justice. Dzurgba argues:

> The individual is loyal to the state because he is a member of the state who enjoys its provisions of gratifications. Thus, what serves the interest of the state serves the interest of the individual, what threatens the state threatens the individual also. This is the core of the essence of the national loyalty on the part of the individual.[16]

This is the individual's loyalty to the state and in response to this on the part of government, Dzurgba comments:

---

13. Dzurgba, *Nigerian Politics and Moral Behaviour*, 41.
14. Dzurgba, 41.
15. Dzurgba, 42.
16. Dzurgba, 42.

A government can be "the best" government, if it creates a moral behaviour which can induce the individual to attain a high degree of sense of responsibility, accountability, efficiency and productivity in the pursuit of interests which can enrich his life. It liberates the energy of the individual for effective performance of his duty. It gives a maximum scope for free interchange of ideas and creates most favourable conditions for people to express their moral attitudes of love, sympathy, mercy, ...[17]

This strong moral consciousness and behavior, Dzurgba believes, will help "minimize anarchic and fraudulent tendencies" and thus promote our "effective pursuit of excellence in all fields" within the state.[18] It is obvious in these data that actual practical politics, when it is direct, serves in its own right as an ethical foundation. Thus, moral values are essential in participatory politics. But the authors under review fail to tell us *how* moral values, ethical principles, or moral integrity can be attained in practical politics. How do we develop moral principles and apply them in politics? Failure to answer these questions by these authors makes the focus of this book relevant. Could religion have anything to offer in politics in light of moral integrity? This will lead us to the next segment of the review: *religion helps to develop moral integrity in politics*.

Politics and Religion

We propose here that religion has an obligation to do its part in the formation of the moral and political conscience. In the following paragraphs, we will discuss the ideology of further scholars who wrote on politics and religion.

J. Lewis

Lewis in his article, "The Church and Formation of Political Conscience," emphasizes that God is concerned for the whole human being. There is no area that can be marked "off limits" to God. His concern, throughout Scripture, is for the whole human for the whole of life. Thus government has its place in the divine order (Rom 13). Responsibility for government is one of humankind's most important areas of obedience to God. Aspirants of any religion are accountable to him for it. Lewis asserts that the political realm is the one

---

17. Dzurgba, 42.
18. Dzurgba, 42.

structure of social relationships that is all-encompassing.[19] All citizens of every state, Christians and non-Christians alike, are already involved. Christian involvement, therefore, in political life is a Christian responsibility. Lewis says, "A person cannot be a good Christian unless he is a good citizen . . . if a person is not deeply involved in the political life of his or her nation, state and community he or she is a sorry Christian."[20]

R. Gill

In his book, *A Textbook of Christian Ethics*, Gill buttresses the point made by Lewis as regards to Christian involvement in politics. According to him, the problem of the relationship of Christianity to the political order and to issues of social and economic justice is not simply of theoretical interest, but of considerable practical importance. Gill stresses further that at the individual level, the Christian attempts to arrive at an understanding of the implications of his or her faith for involvement in political realities. At the corporate level, ecclesiastical institutions attempt to decide how far they are to be involved in political institutions and political decision-making. "Political regimes are always divinely appointed, even when they conflict with Christian ideals and principles."[21] Thus, Gill says, Christian ethics makes demands upon politicians and political regimes, which are frequently ignored.[22]

O. Abogunrin

The above authors wrote from a Western view, but Nigerian authors are not left out in the debate. Abogunrin in his article, "Religion and Democracy in Nigeria," acknowledges that religion plays a vital role in the daily lives of the people of Nigeria. It has to a large extent influenced the political, economic, social, and moral development of the nation. Religion, according to him, cannot be disregarded by any Nigerian leader, whether military or civil. He notes that successive Nigerian leaders have used religion as an instrument for playing the divide-and-rule game, rather than as a uniting force in a religiously and culturally pluralistic country.[23]

---

19. Lewis, "Church and Formation of Political Conscience," 191–204, https://journals.sagepub.com/doi/10.1177/003463737607300208.
20. Lewis, "Church and Formation," 191.
21. Gill, *Textbook of Christian Ethics*, 144.
22. Gill, 143–144.
23. Abogunrin, "Religion and Democracy in Nigeria," 1–18.

Abogunrin stresses further that humankind is a community builder. Men and women are meant to extend God's love, goodness, and riches of life flowing from him. Creation is actually God wanting to share his divine life and to extend it by creating humankind in his own image. Men and women in turn are meant to establish this community of life. Since human beings are community builders, they have no choice but to be involved in the public arena of human existence.

God immersed himself in the human condition, in the human task, with its historical brokenness. In Jesus Christ, God grappled directly with the anti-normative situation in the political governmental structure to which Christ was inescapably related as a member of the society. The structural pattern was part of the overall structure of the Roman Empire, which was linked to the entire world politics of the period. Abogunrin asserts that the teachings of Jesus had point-blank political implications from which anyone who calls himself or herself a Christian cannot run.[24] He writes, "In many respects his [Christ's] teachings were direct responses to the concrete political problems, political possibilities, political responsibilities and political alternatives which He fearlessly confronted on a daily basis."[25] In other words, Christ's teaching can promote political integrity in any nation.

J. O. Awolalu

Awolalu sees religion from a pluralistic point of view as a sensitive subject which, if handled well, can play a predominant role in preserving the highest ideals in society and in discouraging immorality among its members. He opines that a state is made up of people who govern and are governed. If the people who constitute the state belong to different religious traditions, and all religions have high ideals, one should see the high standard of morality in religion brought into the administration of the state. Awolalu urges religious people to stop and ask themselves: How can we relate religious teachings to the needs of the state? Can a Christian or a Muslim be actively involved in the administration of the state? To Awolalu, religious pluralism is more a factor of strength than of weakness in politics of Nigeria.[26] He stresses:

> When carefully handled, religious pluralism is more a factor of strength than of weakness in nation building. We do not want to

---

24. Abogunrin.
25. Abogunrin, 18.
26. Awolalu, "Religion and State," 8.

build up treasures that will be destroyed by Vandals. How do we ensure a morally good government? Surely we cannot have one without morally good leaders. And how do we ensure a morally good citizenry? For us to have good, responsible leadership and fellowship, religious men and women should go into politics, take part in the administration of the states, rebuke evil, and uphold the highest ideals.[27]

Even though his ideal of religious pluralism is questionable, Awolalu agrees that religious ideals cannot be separated from politics. Awolalu believes that religious people are morally sound for politics hence he encourages them to be involved.

Taiye Adamolekun

Religion as a changing factor in the spiritual, political, and social life of any society is stressed by Adamolekun. Religion is relevant to the development of every facet of human life and can serve as a springboard for the inculcation and improvement of moral values, which are fundamental to political modernization, productivity, and nation building. This, he says, is greatly needed in decadent contemporary Nigerian society.[28]

He examines ethics and morality as a code of conduct in the three major religions in Nigeria – Christianity, Islam and African Traditional Religion. He observes that these major religions in Nigeria have similarities in their ethical codes and that this could be taken as an encouragement and possible impetus for the quest of a political and ethical re-orientation of Nigeria. He states, "the civilization of their respective ethical norms by different religious adherents can result in the development of the physical, mental, psychological and spiritual potentials of humans, and can facilitate effective nation building in all its ramifications."[29]

Emile Durkheim and Max Weber

Adamolekun recommends the philosophies of Emile Durkheim and Max Weber, together with the moral and ethical codes of Nigerian religions, as a solution to the national socio-political and ethical life. These sociologists confirm that religion is a source of morality. Religion has nothing to show

---

27. Awolalu, 8.
28. Adamolekun, "Role of Religion," 19.
29. Adamolekun, 21.

society in practical terms when it has no power to produce moral character in society. Religion is not merely about believing, it is also an influence in character. Religion that plays no role in human society is worthless. Religion must have sufficient impact on human life to satisfy to the fullest one's hopes and desires.[30]

In the political scene, Adamolekun emphasizes that religion should serve as an agent of cohesion and stability and asserts that Emile Durkheim's philosophy of religion as an agent of cohesion in society should be followed to curb immoral behavior. He also says that Max Weber's idea of hard work as a divine calling should be adopted. Adamolekun believes that if the ideas of Durkheim and Weber are put into practice, the political life of Nigeria will change for the better – socially, morally, and ethically.[31]

M. O. Adeleye

Adeleye also asserts that religion has a place in human society. His assertion is that religion in society creates good citizens who in turn create healthy politics. He believes that religion has a place in all social institutions in that it helps members of society both socially and politically. "A well-fused religion and politics will not only format and produce a good society but will cement the interest of the society and transfer the austerity of a nation to a real prosperity."[32] He stresses further that politics and religion are inseparable. "The world will become too dull if there is no politics which is the basis of the administrative set up of the society. In like manner the world will be full of vices and evils if there is no religion and men's thoughts will be vulgar and feelings vain . . . The Laws of the nation emanated from the laws of God."[33] Thus, Adeleye concludes that the absence of religion in politics causes a lack of order and regulations with which to guide the populace. This only leads to disorderliness, foulness, and recklessness. Implicitly, Adeleye has in mind that religious teachings produce moral values in politics.

J. O. Akao

In his article, "Christianity and the Quest for Democracy,"[34] Akao opines that Christianity is inseparable from politics; that religion and politics have over

---

30. Adamolekun, 21.
31. Adamolekun, 21.
32. Adeleye, "Religion, Politics and Society," 64.
33. Adeleye, 73.
34. Akao, "Christianity and the Quest for Democracy in Nigeria," 53–58.

the ages remained two inseparable twins. In reference to the Old Testament, he said that if God is himself interested and involved in the earthly governance of his people, there should be nothing wrong if his children continue the work he started. Religion has much to contribute to both the spiritual and physical well-being of humanity and the society in which they live. Akao agrees with Plato who said, "A nation cannot be strong unless it believes in God. Religion has an important contribution to make to the moral strength and the political unity of the nation."[35] Thus, Akao urges:

> Because politics is so important, touching virtually every facet of human life, it will be tantamount to abdication of responsibility for Christians to leave it to self-vaunted professionals, irrespective of their social status, moral stature or credit-worthiness.[36]

He believes that if the Christian principles of social ethics and stewardship of wealth are imbibed, the plundering of the national treasury and the misappropriation of public funds will cease. Thus, he encourages Christians to adhere to, by example, this divine principle from the private to the public sector.[37] Akao observes that the Nigerians' quest for democracy on its own cannot solve our national problems; the belief that attaining democratic status with party politics, will resolve all political, social, economic, and cultural problems and imbalances. Experience has shown that it takes more than a free and fair election, as well as the choice of the right candidate, to transform the individual and society.[38]

Democratic electoral processes in themselves, according to Akao, no matter how free and fair, can never guarantee the dawn of a golden age in any nation. Thus, he said, "the realization of the dreams of the populace lies in the integrity of those who service the political system."[39] It is on this assertion that Akao encourages the transformed children of God with their spiritual enablement to step into Nigerian politics in order "to stop making our democratic process a market place where people can buy and sell votes, mortgage their conscience, trade in their ethnic identity or fan the embers of conspiracy, inordinate ambition, deceit, violence or intimidation."[40] Thus,

---

35. Akao, 53.
36. Akao, 55.
37. Akao, 58.
38. Akao, 58.
39. Akao, 56.
40. Akao, 57.

a well-meaning religious person or a Christian who is not prepared to help arrest these vices has no business going into party politics.

Yusuf Ameh Obaje

Obaje not only recognizes the role of religion in politics, but he advocates for a non-democratic system of government for Nigeria, which causes people to refer to him as a "savior." To him, democracy is rooted in a purely humanistic philosophy and devoid of any spiritual foundation. Democracy therefore is people-centered and has no place for God. "It is equally disturbing to note that in our attempt to import the democracy of the West, we have declared in our constitution that Nigeria is a secular state in spite of the fact that in reality Nigeria is a multi-religious state."[41] Obaje believes that religion is of supreme importance to the survival of any state. He stresses that "democracy as a form of government which focuses purely on people without any serious reference to God is atheistic in its philosophical stance and it is therefore not suitable for a deeply religious people like Nigerians."[42]

He believes that the formation and running of an enduring and prosperous government is one in partnership with God. To him, "any attempt to develop a political system which claims viability and relevance to the people must take into consideration: Who God is, the nature of the particular people who are to live by the political system, their relationship with God and their worldview."[43]

In other words, Obaje believes that God as the Creator, sustainer, supreme judge, and ultimate controller of events and people cannot be ignored, imagined out of existence, or brushed aside by any human institution or system without the resulting negative consequences. In fact, Obaje, a professor of Systematic Theology and Christian Philosophy, was a prominent figure in Obasanjo administration. Obaje experimented with his belief about politics in relation to the Almighty God when he became the chaplin. President Obasanjo appointed Prof. Obaje as the chaplin of Government House in Aso-Rock, Abuja. On a daily basis in Government House for the first time, Jesus Christ, the Son of God, was being preached to the Executive Arms of the Government, in particular in Aso-Rock Chapel initiated by Obaje. Obaje was special adviser to the President on religious matters.

---

41. Obaje, *Theonicracy and Not Democracy for Nigeria*, 16.
42. Obaje, 17.
43. Obaje, 36.

Conclusion

A critical review of these data reveals that while all these authors have made different contributions to the study of politics in relation to ethics and religion, none has truly made an in-depth study of integrity, particularly in Nigerian politics. This validates the relevance and significance of the research in this book in focusing on the field of Christian social ethics. In the next chapter, the ecology and practice of the Nigerian political society will be treated in the light of moral investigation.

3

A Historical Survey of Nigerian Political Society

Aristotle, in the opening pages of his *Politics*, reminds us that "every community is established with a view to some good" which he describes as a "good life."[1] In itself, the phrase is not a univocal concept since "good life" means different things to different societies and political communities. The objectives and aims of one society are not exactly those of another.[2] In Nigerian politics, to understand the "good" aimed for by the community, or what constitutes a "good life" for its citizens – and above all the means to it – one has to look at the meaning of politics in the light of the Bible (as discussed in the last chapter) and the nature of politics in Nigeria, its past and current political affairs. In other words, we take a brief look at past Nigerian politics and the way it governs the people in their struggles for a "good life."

The moral vices in Nigerian democratic politics did not begin with the present administration; therefore, to find a lasting solution to the problem, the past life of the nation cannot be overlooked. Thus this chapter examines briefly but realistically the nature of politics in Nigeria and the basic moral issues under which it has hitherto labored. It is not misleading or out of context to analyze morally the formative years of Nigeria as a nation-state. (Though in the consequent chapters, the evaluation will be strictly limited to Obasanjo democratic government.) We begin with pre-colonial Nigeria, that is, the native people or tribes that made up present Nigeria.

---

1. As quoted in Okolo, *Philosophy and Nigerian Politics*, 7.
2. Okolo, 7–8.

Pre-Colonial Politics in Nigeria

Nothing can be understood about Nigerian politics until its pattern of tribal and ethnic diversity is delineated. Within the boundaries drawn by the British are a staggering variety of tribes and sub-tribes with strong tribal authority and nationalism.[3] "Tribe" here refers to those people who have a common name for their language and feel themselves to be "on the same page" irrespective of the present political circumstances. The traditional authority within these numerous tribes lies in the indigenous leadership of tribal chiefs, emirs, Oba or Obi, who not only seek to integrate tribal sanctions with secular sanctions but also lay emphasis upon traditional forms of social and political life.[4] These tribes are made up of about 248 distinct languages; however, many of these linguistic groups are tiny and politically insignificant. But each of these people has a tribal nationalism or "a political theory which tends to strengthen the position of traditional authority and to retard the effort of nationalism as a unifying factor to achieve self-government for the whole country."[5] Let's examine briefly the various major tribal societies and their political lives and factors that disrupt the traditional societies.

Pre-Colonial Tribal Societies

During this era, people were divided into numerous tribes, great and small, speaking different languages, worshipping various divinities and gods, and differing one from another in manners and customs. Of the origin of these people little is known. The aborigines "have left practically no written records or monuments, and their traditions, interwoven with myth and legend, are fragmentary and in many cases conflicting."[6] "Wave after wave of invasion appears to have swept over the country," and the weaker tribes have been driven back and "scattered by successive conquerors."[7]

There are, however, three major tribal groups that dominated in the pre-colonial period: namely, the Hausa-Fulani, predominantly inhabiting the north; the Yoruba, inhabiting the southwest; and the Igbo living in the southeastern part of the country. But besides these three major tribes, there are several other linguistic groups, or tribes and sub-tribes, such as the Edo,

---

3. Diamond, *Class, Ethnicity and Democracy in Nigeria*, 21.
4. Ezera, *Constitutional Developments in Nigeria*, xv.
5. Diamond, *Class, Ethnicity and Democracy in Nigeria*.
6. Burns, *History of Nigeria*, 39.
7. Burns, 39.

Kanuri, Tiv, Nupe, Ibibio, Itsekiris, Urhobos, Anang, Ijaws, Gwaris, Igalas, and others.[8] The northern Nigerian people belong to an area geographically and historically known as the Western Sudan. Bordering upon the southern section of the Sahara and typically consisting of open savannah, it was tied to North Africa and through it to the Middle East for centuries before the European "discoveries" of West Africa. Waves of migrating people had come to West Africa from North Africa and perhaps the Middle East.[9]

The legends of the origin of some of the southern Nigerian people like the Yoruba also tell of migrations from North Africa or the Middle East, and some of them felt the influence of Islam and Arab culture through the Northern people. The Yoruba myths trace their origin to Ile-Ife, a town in the center of the Yoruba nation. The Igbo point out that linguistically they belong to the Sudanese family, but their origin is not precisely known except for speculations based on certain cultural similarities which point to a distant connection with the Near East. These various tribes, north and south of Nigeria, exhibited tribal politics even before British colonialism.[10]

Pre-Colonial Tribal Politics

A common political history can help hold a nation together, but the most significant general comment that can be made about pre-colonial politics in Nigeria is that it is not Nigerian politics but rather tribal politics, that is, politics of different tribes or groupings of tribes with instituted traditional authority.[11] Pre-colonial Nigeria exhibited independent and dependent cultural nations.[12] A variety of links existed between the various states and people which were the predecessors of modern Nigeria. But some of those links were with neighboring peoples; not all were Nigerian. Some scholars classify them into two ideological and societal types – the centralized and non-centralized. The centralized tribes include the Yoruba, Fulani and Kanem Bornu empires, Benin kingdom, Hausa states and Igbo chiefdoms. These were governed by ruling classes based on *divine kingship*. Rulership in the non-centralized tribes was based on age and religious status. Therefore political rewards varied from tribe to tribe.[13]

---

8. Ezera, *Constitutional Developments in Nigeria*, 2.
9. Schwarz Jr., *Nigeria: The Tribes, the Nation, or the Race*, 6–10.
10. Schwarz Jr., 6–10; Ezera, *Constitutional Developments in Nigeria*, 4–10.
11. W. Schwarz, *Nigeria*, 12.
12. Olatunji, "Public Accountability and Nation Building," 96.
13. Olatunji, 96.

For many years the Hausa were politically dominant in the north. Later the Fulani empire took over through Muslim jihad. Thus under the *theocratic government* of their Fulani rulers, the peoples of this area were divided politically into various states. This Hausa-Fulani diffusion greatly affected their social and political organizations especially with regards to Islamic laws and doctrines. "By virtue of their religion and their theocentric government, the [Hausa-Fulani] have become a well-disciplined people, one of whose characteristic features is unquestioning obedience to constituted authority."[14]

The Yoruba kingdom has a comparatively large scale of political organization and the tradition of *constitutional monarchy* which they possessed long before the advent of the British. Yoruba tribal politics was that of a constitutional monarchy built upon overlapping family, lineage, and clan units. At the center of a Yoruba state there was an Oba, or a king, but substantial power was also held by the heads of families or clans, and sub-chiefs, who did not owe their office to the Oba. This type of monarchical political tradition is practiced in Yoruba land, the Islamic north, Benin, and some other places.[15]

A larger part of Igbo tribes and sub-tribes, and other tribes especially in the East, practice a *traditional democratic government* or consultative method of political decision-making.[16] They "have had no indigenous overall political authority around which their loyalty was crystallized. The basic social unit among them is the family or a kindred composed of such families and the largest political unit has normally been the village group."[17] Some areas, however, had a tradition of *hereditary chiefdom*. Men and women have organizations (age-groups) based on their dates of birth and marriage, and these societies transcend village groups and even community or clan boundaries.[18] The traditional political process in this part of the country, is that for public matters to be discussed at a general meeting every able-bodied male who is a full member of the community has a right to attend and to speak if he so wishes. After a general discussion the elders retire to consult and when they return a spokesman announces their decision to the meeting who either accept it by general acclamation or refuse it.[19]

---

14. Ezera, *Constitutional Developments in Nigeria*, 5.
15. Ezera, 5–6.
16. W. Schwarz, *Nigeria*, 31–32.
17. Ezera, *Constitutional Developments in Nigeria*, 8.
18. Ezera, 8.
19. W. Schwarz, *Nigeria*, 33.

Disruption of Tribal Societies

There are three major external forces that disrupted Nigeria's traditional societies and their various locally established political authorities. They are *Islam*, *Christianity*, and *secular Western civilization*, which broke apart the various kingdoms, empires, and nations of pre-colonial societies. Converts to Islam and Christianity have a bond with their co-religionists that cuts across ethnic lines. Both universal religions brought with them the tools and skills to widen men's and women's horizons beyond their tribal boundaries. For instance, these faiths are responsible for writing in Nigeria: with Islam came the Arabic script in the north; Christian missionaries in the south first put the southern languages into writing, and they taught English as well. With Western influences came a more sophisticated cash economy and a belief in individual liberty, both of which reduced the tribal bond of the traditional societies. But while those external forces have reduced tribal differences in some ways, they have also reinforced them in others. Their impact has created a wide divergence between north and south which is a debilitating drain upon the vitality of Nigerian national integrity, since it cuts across tribal lines.

Similarly, Western secular ideas have affected Nigeria's ethnicities with many variables. Due to the fact that modern power depends largely upon acquisition of the skills of the West, new tensions have been induced into the "blood of Nigerians." The Yoruba, for example, were the first to embrace Western education, which has a wider and deeper spread among them than other tribes in Nigeria.[20]

In a nutshell, this new development among the traditional nations has both positive and negative effects on Nigerian politics. The fact remains that these various tribes still maintain their separate identities and this raises serious political conflicts, especially in the post-colonial period. The nature of these conflicts is understood better when it is realized that for most Nigerians, patriotic feelings are purely local and inspired by tribal loyalties. It is also paramount to note that in Nigeria one cannot become part of a tribe – one is born into it. One can settle in a village and become part of the community, but cannot become part of the tribe that owns it.[21]

This tribal situation brought about a narrow and local approach to political issues in Nigerian politics. Kalu Ezera rightly observes that "tribal loyalties and local feelings still becloud the attitude of most Nigerian political leaders and their disciples. These tribal leanings have prevented, to a large extent, the

---

20. W. Schwarz, *Nigeria*, 6.
21. Ezera, *Constitutional Developments in Nigeria*, 11.

emergence of national loyalties, patriotic integrity, and country-wide political parties."[22] These cleavages of tribe, religion, habits, and language are, in many cases, so deep-seated, especially among Nigerian leaders, that it has proven to be a difficult task to bridge them before British colonial rule gave way to self-government.[23] This will be evidenced as we discuss briefly colonial politics in Nigeria.

Colonial Politics in Nigeria

The geographic entity called "Nigeria" today is, indeed, a British imperial creation. The formative years of modern African nations, Nigeria inclusive, started in the late 1880s. The scramble for Africa by the European nations almost resulted in an inter-imperialist war. "To remedy the situation, the German chancellor Otto Von Bismarck convened a diplomatic summit of European powers in the late nineteenth century. This summit became known as the Berlin West Africa Conference (BWAC)."[24] So the concept of "African nations" as we have it today, was conceived in the later part of nineteenth century by the European nations in Berlin meeting between November 1884 and February 1885 when the autonomous African peoples were divided and shared among themselves into political units.[25] With the Berlin Act, Africa, the home of "dark people," became the home of the "white people" who swarmed like wild locusts in their hundreds and thousands across the entire continent, a land flowing with milk and honey, and ravaged it over several decades until the appointed time when the "black people" cried to the "colorless God," the Creator of the universe. With his intervention, Africans made a move to regain control of their land.

Modern Nigeria's existence came about in the early twentieth century, when Lord Lugard conquered the Muslim emirates in what constitutes northern Nigeria today.[26] After this, many British stayed behind. Colonial rule left a new country with a measure of both political and economic unity, but the British did more to unify the country economically than politically. The political unity that developed later stemmed much more from the natives' assimilation of alien ideas and their collective desire to oust alien politicians than from any design

---

22. Ezera, 11.
23. Ezera, 12.
24. Luka, *Jesus Christ as Ancestor*, 44.
25. Obasanjo, "New Year's Message – Broadcast on NTA," 259.
26. Ezera, *Constitutional Developments in Nigeria*, 12.

of the colonists. Even the economic aspect of development was in the interest of the British and not for the benefit of the tribal nations. Racial prejudice and class snobbery marred the British records.[27]

The British acquisition of the tribal nations kept the peace in a land that had been beset by tribal wars. They imported new and more just means of administration. They built a modern network of roads across the tribes. Certain policies instituted by the British showed the growth of a politically cohesive country. Indirect rule perpetuated tribal differences and favored the traditional aristocracy as opposed to a new class free of tribal shackles. The isolation of the northern part of Nigeria from disruptive influences that were transforming their southern counterpart left the northerners backwards, fearful, and resentful, and the southern tribes scornful of the northern tribes. The aftermath of this tension has distorted and plagued Nigerian politics and made national integration and integrity infinitely harder.[28]

British politics in Nigeria, however, facilitated the birth of new ideas such as secularism, federalism, democracy, and nationalism. These imported ideas, to a large extent, provide an atmosphere conducive to a new way of perceiving and relating to "intra-and inter-religious-ethnic disjunction."[29] A brief review of the main stages in the development of the colonial polices in Nigeria may be helpful to gain an understanding of the issue of Nigerian politics and moral integrity. Indeed this review may help to show that modern Nigeria did not spring into being as a complete whole, politically and administratively. There was a tendency to centralized administration in her pre-natal stage of life but political unity was not attempted until sometime later.

Formative Years of Modern Nigeria

As stated above, the concept of "Nigeria" as a nation was conceived in the later part of the nineteenth century by the European nations in Berlin in the 1884–1885 Conference. In that BWAC meeting "the autonomous African peoples were forcefully divided and separated by a stroke of the pen, merged into political units without empirical justification."[30] The British penetration into the ethnic groups of modern Nigeria, however, dates back to the days of the slave trade. Ezera notes that the British presence may be attributable to

---

27. W. Schwarz, *Nigeria*, 23.
28. W. Schwarz, 29.
29. Singh, "Analysis of Mawlawa Mawdudi's Political Theory," 123.
30. Obasanjo, "New Year's Message – Broadcast on NTA," 259.

three main groups of activities, namely: trade at the mouth of the river Niger; the proselytizing zeal of Christian missions; and the British government's determined effort to suppress the traffic in slaves.[31] On these notes one can say that the British were on God's mission consciously or unconsciously. This is because the "finger of God" is obvious in the creation of Nigeria and its political development.

The British colonization of Nigeria started in Lagos colony in 1850 and was completed in 1903 with military expeditions that crushed the invincibility of the former Sokoto caliphate. The management of the emergent political system was administered under two protectorate systems: the Northern and Southern protectorates.[32] Thirty years after the decision of the Berlin conference in 1884, Nigeria as a united country was born on 1 January 1914.[33] It was the amalgamation of the two protectorates that gave rise to the formation of modern Nigeria as a nation. Lord Lugard, who championed the amalgamation, became the first governor-general of the colony and protectorate of Nigeria. And it was Lord Lugard who introduced into Nigeria the system of indirect rule.[34] For a period of forty-six years, Nigeria had been under British colonial political governance. Lugard created modern Nigeria in 1914 and it is only from that point, that any reference to what is today called "Nigeria" can, strictly speaking, begin.

Formation of Nigerian Political Crisis

The governing system for the amalgamated Nigeria was federal in character in that it recognized the existence of two autonomous parts called the Northern and Southern Provinces. A lieutenant-governor was placed over each part of the nation with direct administrative power over the area of appointment. The headquarters for the lieutenant-governor of Northern Nigeria was located at Kaduna, while that of Southern Nigeria was located at Lagos. The headquarters of the governor-general was also established in Lagos.[35] In 1947 when the Richards Constitution came into effect, Nigeria was further divided into three

---

31. Ezera, *Constitutional Developments in Nigeria*, 13.
32. Albert, "Federalism, Inter-Ethnic Conflicts," 50–51.
33. Awolalu, "Religion and National Unity," 2.
34. Ezera, *Constitutional Developments in Nigeria*, 15.
35. Ezera, 20.

regions: North, West, and East.[36] Since that point, Nigerians have struggled for nationhood in the face of internal reaction and external interference.[37]

The Richards Constitution escalated tribal conflict in Nigeria due to the fact that before its implementation the country was ruled by two separate and contradictory systems. In the northern part of Nigeria, the political system was controlled by traditional rulers (emirs) in fulfilment of the promise Lord Lugard made to Lamido of Adamawa and the Sultan of Sokoto in 1901 and 1903 respectively. Lugard promised the emirs that he would not tamper with the existing religious-political systems in that part of the country. It was on this treaty that the policy of indirect rule was woven, which was very popular in colonial northern Nigeria.[38]

But southern Nigeria, on the other hand, had representatives in the national legislative assembly and so was more sophisticated politically than the northern Nigerians. Western education and Christianity were also not as successful in the north; in the south they were vigorously promoted and English was employed as the administrative language.[39] Institutionalized regionalism in Nigerian politics was not in favor of nationalism; rather British imperialists aimed at preserving their colonial interests through direct rule and through a divide-and-rule system by the establishment of different legislatures for each region. The constitution institutionalized tribal nationalism and competitive regional politics in Nigeria.[40] It thus compounded the mutual suspicion between the different ethnic groups in the country and marked the genesis of acrimonious ethnic loyalties in Nigerian politics. British colonial politics failed to develop institutions that could have integrated Nigeria around common cultural, social, and political symbols and structures.[41]

The deepening regionalism manifested itself in the three political parties that were established around this time. They took steps to entrench themselves in their predominant cultural regions – the Northern People's Congress (NPC) for Hausa-Fulani northerners, the Action Group (AG) for Yoruba-dominated western Nigeria, and the National Congress of Nigerian Citizens (NCNC) for the Igbo-dominated eastern region. Each of the groups or parties became

---

36. Albert, "Federalism, Inter-Ethnic Conflicts," 50.
37. Sangosanya, *Emirate Council and Politics*, 2.
38. Albert, "Federalism, Inter-Ethnic Conflicts," 50.
39. Albert, 51.
40. Sangosanya, *Emirate Council and Politics*.
41. Diamond, *Class, Ethnicity and Democracy*, 28.

the instruments for protecting the parochial interest of particular tribes.[42] The predominance of the three major tribes is amplified by their regional concentration in the country. The sharp differences in the traditional cultures and social structures between the Hausa-Fulani, Igbo, and Yoruba gave their numerical preponderance political significance. The regional structure gave these three major tribes, and their political cultures and aspirations, dominant political roles in each of their regions, substantially exaggerating the centralized character of tribal structure.[43]

In national politics, each of the three major ethnic groups feared the domination of one another. The Yoruba feared the Igbo; the Igbo feared the Yoruba; the Yoruba and Igbo (who constituted the southerners) were feared by the northerners, and vice versa. The political leaders of the three parties, who should have promoted nationalism, inflamed the fear of domination.[44] Even within each region there was no political peace. Each region contained significant ethnic minorities who, fearing and resenting the dominance of the major ethnic groups in the region, agitated for greater autonomy. While these minority tribes were each relatively small, collectively they amounted to more than a third of the Nigerian population, and while they were politically fragmented, they constituted in each region a strategic political constituency. The demographic balance of tribal groups within each region thus became a significant factor to be reckoned with in Nigeria's politics.[45] The political tension between minorities and majorities in Nigerian politics during colonial rule was best observed by Larry Diamond:

> A different ethnic cleavage in Nigeria found the various ethnic minority groups rising in opposition to the dominance of the major group in each region. The political organisation of ethnic minorities gathered momentum in the twilight of colonial rule, fed by mounting apprehension of political repression, socio-economic discrimination, even cultural extinction by the majority groups when they took unfettered control of regional governments after Independence. Seeking for their people safe-guards against such abuse, and for themselves power and its material fruits, minority-group politicians spawned movements for separate states that, if

---

42. Albert, "Federalism, Inter-Ethnic Conflicts."
43. Diamond, *Class, Ethnicity and Democracy*, 23.
44. Albert, "Federalism, Inter-Ethnic Conflicts."
45. Diamond, *Class, Ethnicity and Democracy*, 24.

successful, would have totally transformed the existing regional structure.[46]

Thus, since the 1957 constitutional conference, these minority groups' demand for separate states had become the most explosive issue in Nigerian politics. Elites from the various minority groups of each of the three regions demanded their separate states – the Ibibio, Efik, Ijaws and other non-Igbo ethnic minority groups in the southeast; Edo, Urhobos and others in the southwest; and the Yorubas in Kabba and Ilorin, and the Kanuri, Tiv and others of the Middle Belt in the north. The minority's fears and grievances centered around obtaining a "fair" share of the rewards of an expanding economy and state, such as contracts, loans, scholarships, processing plants, water supplies, street lights, schools, and hydroelectric projects. The minority's demands for separate states were based on the fact that they were being cheated in the distribution of these resources by the regional governments, and that the existing modest restraints on this oppression would evaporate with the departure of the British. It is clear that the mobilization and statehood demands of the minorities also reflected deep emotional attachments, just like their majority's counterparts, to their distinctive groups' values, languages, ways of life, and historical traditions. Indeed, it was a genuine fear that their cultural distinctiveness would be suppressed or obliterated. In spite of this obvious fear of intimidation and repression all over the country, the British opposed the creation of any new states.[47]

At one level of analysis, the political crisis in Nigeria during the colonial period and beyond was largely the product of the convergence of tribes as well as regional and political divisions. Political motivation was based on "tribalhood" and not "nationhood." Every tribe sought the interest of their own people to the detriment of Nigerian collective politics that would promote justice, mutual trust, tolerance, and equity. The colonial politics was characterized by politics of self-interest, which was first initiated by the colonialists and then followed by the tribalists. Thus, the political formation of Nigeria was laid with the "building blocks" of political intrigue and bloodshed – "nationalist aspirations turned into inter-regional, inter-ethnic and inter-party antagonism and mutual distrust."[48] Though this was controlled relatively well by the British government, it escalated after independence. British colonial

---

46. Diamond, 52.
47. Diamond, 54.
48. Osadolor, "Development of the Federal Idea," 45.

politics established tribal nationalism, which only strengthened the position of various ethnic authorities and slowed the effort of true nationalism, which ought to have been a unifying factor in achieving self-government in Nigerian politics without much tension.

In a nutshell, economic investment was the driving factor of British colonial politics. The development of industrialization and capitalism were the principal motives of colonialism. As a result of this, the setting up of political authority was not necessarily to introduce a new governing system in Nigeria, but rather to secure the necessary structures that would enable investments to yield high dividends.[49] Thus, colonial politics was an investment in Nigerian societies. This was the political ideology sold to the neo-colonialists, whether civilians or military officers, who also saw politics as an investment.

Independence Politics in Nigeria

At the stroke of midnight on that memorable day, 1 October 1960, the green and white flag of the Federal Republic of Nigeria was raised for the first time in the political epoch of the world. In a serene atmosphere remarkable for its subdued character and "quiet constitutional dignity," Nigeria was formally granted her independence. The ceremonies and speeches dignified the manner in which successive British governments have gradually transformed leadership responsibilities to bona fide Nigerians. The prime minister of the "new weaned nation" expressed the quiet optimism and sobriety with which Nigerians accepted their birth as a nation.

Nigeria's independent political era has had only a short history. In colonial days, the liberal nationalists saw themselves as Africans rather than Nigerians. Later, when independence became a real prospect, they conceived themselves as West Africans, with the hope of a West African Federation. But under divine inspiration in 1897, Flora Shaw, "the mother of Nigeria" who was betrothed to Lord Lugard, coined the word "Nigeria," and the word became a nation after "seventeen years of pregnancy" in 1914. Thus, Nigeria was born as an African nation. Indeed, a feeling of Nigeria nationhood did develop with the advent of independence. But the end of the anti-colonialism was the beginning of "politics"; and what was politics? Just tribalism. What else was the moral justification for independence? The only real radicalism had been against the British. Now that the British were gone, the main thing was

---

49. Adeniran, "Colonial Rule and Factors of Development," 18.

how to share a limited "national cake."⁵⁰ The politics of wealth and position was the ideology of most politicians in independent politics. Cowan rightly observes that "colonialism is no longer Nigeria's besetting problem. The old, easily identifiable enemy has, for the most part, been eliminated. In its place has arisen a jumble of complex, elusive, but frighteningly real, problems – the dilemmas of independence."⁵¹ The assessment of the eve of independence will help to understand the political upheaval of the era.

The Eve of Independence

At one level of moral analysis, political conflict in Nigeria during the eve of independence was largely the product of the convergence of ethnic, regional, and political divisions. They sprang from "the struggle among the political classes to continue the narrow resource base of an underdeveloped economy and state, a moral and political struggle which, as it became tribal, ultimately infected the whole of political and social life in Nigeria, even at independence and beyond."⁵² Nigerian politics became one of bartering for socio-economic benefits. For hardened politicians, the gains of politics proved more decisive than altruistic considerations. Changes in imperial policy, as a result of World War II, and the increased quest by Nigerian nationalists for self-government and independence, led to concessions by British officials in the last decade before independence. It was an era of shared responsibility between British and Nigerian officials, a cooperative government, which ushered in Nigerian independence.⁵³

On 12 December 1959, there was a general election throughout the country to determine which of the three main political parties would form the government to receive the British transfer of power – the NCNC, NPC, or AG. The major parties campaigned vigorously throughout the nation, promising the same sort of development and welfare programs.⁵⁴ The election was wrought over personalities rather than politics, and the voting patterns were largely on a tribal basis. During the campaign, the AG leader, Awolowo, hired the services of an American public relations firm, which provided a helicopter that wrote

---

50. W. Schwarz, *Nigeria*, 12; Diamond, *Class, Ethnicity and Democracy*, 64.
51. Cowan, *Dilemmas of African Independence*, cover page.
52. Diamond, *Class, Ethnicity and Democracy*, 45.
53. Tamuno, "Nigerian Federalism in Historical Perspective," 15.
54. Diamond, *Class, Ethnicity and Democracy*, 57.

"Awo" in the sky. This was the genesis of "money politics," big-party spending in Nigerian politics.[55]

The tone of the electoral campaign was morally bankrupt. Crudely, at times hysterically, candidates heaped personal and ethnic abuse upon one another. The AG leader, for instance, accused the NCNC and NPC of "exhibiting dictatorial tendencies of the Hitlerite or Nasserite type," while the NCNC president condemned the AG as "godless worshipers" and "enemies of democracy." Such vitriolic rhetoric marked the electoral display throughout the decade, especially that of "abusive war" between the AG and the NCNC, whose leaders and candidates routinely vilified their counterparts as "jellyfishes in human form," traitors to the nationalist cause, incipient fascists, crooks, liars, "semiliterate," and so forth. Thus, the fanatical and tribalistic tone of 1959 and the entire decade had dangerous moral consequences.[56]

In the 1959 electoral campaign, many things went wrong even though the British controlled the situation to an extent. In a context in which so much was at stake in an election and in which the populous rural and illiterate electorate lacked the sophistication and the breath of exposure to dismiss fantastic charges as mere rhetorical excess, venomous rhetoric bred violence and repression. This was the case in most parts of the country. In the north, especially, the NPC used its control of traditional systems of administration and justice to victimize, obstruct, and punish opposition candidates and their supporters. There was widespread denial of campaign permits, harassment at rallies, and false imprisonment of candidates, which bred hatred of other parties against NPC action. In the south, regional power was deployed with a heavy hand against electoral opposition, and the campaigns there were much more violent. "From the inception of electoral competition in 1951, parties fielded bands of thugs to disrupt, intimidate, and attack the opposition. Injuries in the hundreds were not uncommon."[57] Both in the north and south, election campaigns were exceedingly tough, with cars burnt, semi-riots where the campaign teams converged, and politicians declaring that their lives were in danger.[58]

This was the background of the political unity, or lack thereof, at independence. In spite of this running tension, political leaders were teaming up against one another. From 1957 to 1959, all three parties participated in a joint coalition government (headed by Tafawa Balewa). Hence, the succession

---

55. W. Schwarz, *Nigeria*, 112.
56. Diamond, *Class, Ethnicity and Democracy*, 57–58.
57. Diamond, 58.
58. Diamond, 59.

of political issues over time threw the various interest groups against one another in a shifting rather than cumulative pattern. Therefore, there was continuous variation in outcomes at the eve of independence. No group or party dominated the scene. Each party always won or lost; each enjoyed victory and suffered defeat, and was now and then coaxed or coerced into a compromise by the British authority. But even so, the intensity of crises had reached a dangerous level prior to independence; mutual tolerance, trust, restraint, and respect all waned through the successive electoral struggles and intervening political upheavals.[59] Thus independence was celebrated with mixed feelings among Nigerians.

The National Independence

The celebrations began at midnight on 30 September 1960. In a solemn yet colorful ceremony, Princess Alexandra of Kent, on behalf of Her Majesty Queen Elizabeth II, handed over the constitutional instrument for Nigerian Independence to the Nigerian Prime Minister, Sir Abubaka Tafawa Balewa. By this single act, Nigeria, which had been under the nurture of the British government, was weaned and became an independent nation.[60] Then, at the stroke of midnight on 1 October 1960, the green and white flag of "The Federal Republic of Nigeria" was raised for the first time. The celebrations and speeches gave little emphasis to continuity. Tribute was paid to the manner in which successive British governments had gradually transferred the burden of political responsibility to Nigerians.[61]

The political celebration of Nigeria at independence was a ruse of optimism. The prime minister, Balewa, expressed the quiet hope and sobriety with which Nigerians accepted their birth as a nation. At least for a moment, the bitterness of the eve of independence was submerged in the glow of nationalist pride. In his inaugural address, the governor-general, Azikiwe, took the occasion to appeal to his former rivals to join with him to "bind the nation's wound and heal the breaches of the past."[62] The tone of optimism and hope as a nation was also echoed by foreigners, especially the "Mother Nation," who took considerable pride in leaving behind a functioning parliamentary democratic government.

---

59. Diamond, 62–63.
60. Ezera, *Constitutional Developments in Nigeria*, 265.
61. Diamond, *Class, Ethnicity and Democracy*, 64.
62. Azikiwe quoted in Diamond, 64.

But the depth of the bitterness and rancor of the past was a lot to overcome with the achievement of nationhood. Diamond observes that even as the independence ceremonies were being prepared, and government stalwarts were speaking magnanimously of a new beginning in Nigerian politics, the Federal Opposition leader was threatening the survival of Nigeria as a unitary nation. Diamond writes:

> The Action Group leader was warning his party of threats to its constitutional rule in the Western Region and to its survival as the Federal Opposition, threats that could mean the end of democracy in Nigeria. The continuing enmity and distrust between the Action Group and the two parties of the ruling coalition, the continuing agitation of minority groups for separate states (which the Action Group championed), the high expectations of an impoverished population for rapid economic progress, and the wide and growing gulf between the people and the venal political class, suggested to some that "the optimism of 1960 was justified only in the sense that without optimism there is no hope."[63]

Thus the expectations for Nigerian democracy at independence were generally high, both among Nigerian political stalwarts, and world leaders and observers. But common among nationalists and colonialists was a perception that the worst national division had been laid to rest, that the eve of independence had already demonstrated the viability of democracy in Nigeria.[64]

Perhaps nothing so clouded the future of Nigerian politics as the gross imbalances in values, and the product of another nation's history, of which Awolowo repeatedly and stridently appealed for resolution before independence. The escalating moral repression and harassment it was encountering in the three regions, and the threat it faced at the center made it difficult to classify Nigeria in 1960 as a genuine, democratic, independent nation. "It had a quasi-democratic regime, and was struggling to establish and institutionalise liberal democratic government."[65]

The greatest challenge of the independence era was whether Nigeria is truly a democratic nation or an agglomeration of tribal nations. With all it has been through, is Nigeria still a nation? Was it ever one? Will it survive tribalism? The strengthening of centripetal tendencies seems also to be very

---

63. Diamond, 65.
64. Diamond, 89.
65. Diamond, 89.

powerful, but there are many unresolved social and political issues due to the artificial nature of the country. The exits of any colonial effort to inculcate a sense of nationhood and the deliberate encouragement of regional identities and separation, further worked against the development of a sense of national unity and identity. By independence, the challenge of integrating Nigerian politics around a common, overarching sense of nationhood still remained.[66]

Among the major social and moral catastrophes was gross indiscipline on the part of those who held public offices: embezzlement of public funds, excessive greed, irresponsibility, lack of public accountability, tribalism, nepotism, lack of patriotic spirit, etc. – in a nut-shell, bad political leadership. Mostly it was the nationalists, those highly placed in public offices, who perpetrated these social evils.[67]

Political ruling parties failed to maintain the enthusiasm with which they were swept into power at the time of independence. Moreover, after independence, the political leaders were unable to keep the promises of the better life so rashly made during the anti-colonial struggle. The national unity and identity was threatened even more by the opposition in the western region. The fall of Awolowo as a result of the treason trial and the rise of Akintola, his deputy leader, marked the end of the Action Group as a political party. The catastrophes which emanated from the western region election of 1969 aroused the interest of gunmen into political activities of the country. The final, desperate attempt of the southern alliance to win power by constitutional means, and its failure amid the bitterness of a rigged election, produced the spreading chaos in the west that led directly to the first military coup in Nigeria.[68] Election fever, with its complaints and counter-complaints, its threats and counter-threats, was the rule of game that brought to an end the First Republic politics.[69]

The nation's political independence ceased because most Nigerian political leaders manifested a weak commitment to political moral values and moral lifestyles. For instance, the mottos of the three political parties of the First Nigeria Republic, which guided their respective behavior, testified of their understanding of Nigerian politics. These propaganda-honeyed words also guided their collective social and moral behavior in the forms of alliances and coalitions, and all their political deeds. AG's motto was "Western region

---

66. Diamond, 74.
67. Okolo, *Philosophy and Nigerian Politics*, 12.
68. W. Schwarz, *Nigeria*, 152–179.
69. W. Schwarz, 152–179.

for the westerners, eastern region for the easterners, northern region for the northerners, and Nigeria for all"; the NPC declared "One north, one people, irrespective of religion, rank and tribe"; and the NCNC simply claimed "One Nigeria." It was only the NCNC that portrayed the oneness of Nigerian politics while the others were tribalized or regionalized. These political beliefs were translated into action, which became the sources of the crises in the first Nigerian political scenes that lasted from 1960 to 1966. The independence regime staggered from crisis to crisis and finally came to a close in the coup of 15 January 1966.[70] The question then became whether the military were better able than civilian politicians to run the country, and whether or not they have more acumen and integrity to bring about stability and accountability in Nigeria.

Military Politics in Nigeria

The first phase of party politics in Nigeria lasted from 1951 to 1966, when the military took over for the first time. The story so far paints a gloomy scenario of the tensions and crises that are endemic in Nigerian politics.[71] The increasing violence of political life throughout the country brought military governance onto the political scene of Nigeria. This gloomy scenario of tension, blood shedding, and the destruction of property did not end with the stepping in of the gunmen. May, July, and October of 1966 saw serious outbreaks of rioting in northern Nigeria and the destruction of several lives and properties, mostly Igbo from eastern Nigeria who were residing in northern Nigeria. This resulted in a mass exodus of easterners back to their region, and the rift, which these events produced in the military, led directly to the Nigerian civil war, which lasted for three years. The reunion of eastern Nigeria with the rest of the country was surprisingly peaceful and rapid, and a decade of relative calm descended on Nigerian politics, financed by the oil boom and punctuated only by coups within the military in 1975 and 1976 which led to the fall of Civil War politics under the Gowon junta and the death of a military nationalist, General Murtala Mohammed.[72]

The Nigerian army is a by-product of colonialism and an account of its formation and development cannot but be interwoven with the stages of European contact with the West African coast and its exploration, and

---

70. Dzurgba, *Nigerian Politics and Moral Behaviour*, 47.
71. Agbodike, "Federal Character Principle and National Integration," 181.
72. Eades, "Religion, Politics and Ideology," 181.

exploitation, between the fifteenth and twentieth centuries. Many of the early military officers went directly to Britain for their training. In April 1958 the military forces in Nigeria were handed over to the Nigerian government, meaning the military forces would no longer be under the control of the British junta but by Nigerian civilian government. And by the beginning of 1960, the Nigerian Military Training College, Kaduna, had taken over all skill-training commitments. It was even observed by Obasanjo that the Nigerian army, which was an offshoot of the British colonial army, was supposed to be completely subordinated to civil order. The army is meant to be an apolitical organ of the civil government.[73] But Nigeria has experienced twenty-nine years of military government (1966–1979; 1983–1999) out of the forty-four years of self-government (1960–2004) under review in this book. This section will discuss briefly in two phases the military politics in Nigeria and conclude with a moral assessment.

The First Phase of Military Politics

Military politicians controlled Nigerian politics for thirteen years under the rule of four generals from 1966 to 1979. In the early hours of the morning of 15 January 1966, a section of the Nigerian army, under the command of the late Major C. K. Nzeogwu, revolted in Lagos, Enugu, Ibadan, and Kaduna. Many leading politicians, including the prime minister and the premiers of the north and the west, were killed.[74] Before the military coup, democratic politics had broken down completely in Nigeria and the political system showed every sign of falling apart, therefore only a revolution could resuscitate the country. Government-sponsored papers attacked specific tribal groups, thereby gaining support from other tribes and winning votes. Thugs were used for political coercion; strikes were crippling the economy; riots raged, etc. Unfortunately, the 15 January revolution was aborted by the misguided intervention of those whose ignorance constituted an impediment in the national march as a united people. After all, "revolution means an upheaval, a sudden radical change which seriously affects the people, economic and social system."[75] The aftermath of this aborted revolution was a land littered with the corpses of thousands of men, women, and children, and the collapse of the moral codes,

---

73. Obasanjo, *Nzeogwu*, 34–35.
74. Ojiako, *13 Years of Military Rule*, 3.
75. Nwankwo, *Thoughts on Nigeria*, 69.

the destruction of respect for labor, the breakdown of social values, and the devaluation of human life.[76]

Aguiyi Ironsi stumbled into power in 1966 and tended to toy with the "ripe revolution," mainly because his genuine concern with the apolitical tradition of the Armed Forces poorly prepared him to take up the challenge he had acquired, handed to him on a platter of gold, through the conquest of the inexperienced revolutionists. Indecision commenced when he tried to bargain his revolution-power regime "by arranging a Rump parliament of survivors from the civilian political class to hand over 'constitutional power' to him."[77] In the same vein, Obasanjo comments, "no hired revolutionaries are able to carry out the aims and objectives of a revolution faithfully, satisfactorily and to the letter, while the initiators are bystanders. Revolution by proxy cannot be successful."[78] Aguiyi Ironsi lacked sound moral judgement of the January coup as regards to its hegemonic interpretation. General Ironsi failed to utilize the military moral judgement to stabilize his government against ethnic misconceptions especially between the North and East hegemonies. He was from the east and the northerners were more affected by the military coup hence his coming to the throne was already misinterpreted. His failure to implement the despotic ethics of his military profession contributed to his downfall within five short months of his administration.[79]

On the fourth month of the reign of Aguiyi Ironsi, an announcement of moves towards unitary government was misinterpreted. This sparked off a violent protest demonstration in the north. Easterners were killed and their properties destroyed. The hostility continued and on 29 July 1966, Aguiyi Ironsi along with his military governor Adekunle Fajuyi were assassinated at Ibadan, during a second military coup that brought in the Gowon junta. Again, a number of officers of eastern origin were killed;[80] the aftermath of the military fracas of January and July 1966 resulted in the Nigerian nation splintering into rudderless and hostile groups. It was at this juncture that the mantle of the Gowon junta presided over an unwieldy, complex, and cracking nation. Gowon faced the difficult task of rallying round himself the disillusioned, discredited faction members of the military and civilians, to turn a state of despair into

---

76. Nwankwo, 71–72.
77. Nwankwo, *African Dictators*, 109.
78. Obasanjo, *Nzeogwu*, 100.
79. Nwankwo, *African Dictators*, 109.
80. Ojiako, *13 Years of Military Rule*, 33.

one of hope, and persuade sectionalists and secessionists to regain the vision of one Nigeria.[81]

The Gowon civilian-military junta which set out to stop the nation from drifting into utter destruction, to eradicate corruption, and to organize genuinely national political parties, ended up stumbling into an avoidable civil war, carrying the "sick giant of Africa" through a period of waste and profligacy, and eventually reneged on the promise to return power to the civilian government.[82] In his speech marking the fourteenth anniversary of independence, he dismissed as unrealistic the 1976 deadline for a return to civilian politics:

> Four years ago when I gave 1976 as the target date for returning the country to normal constitutional government, both myself and the military hierarchy honestly believed that by that date, especially after a civil war . . . there would have developed an atmosphere of sufficient stability.[83]

Gowon lamented that Nigerians were not yet ready for democratic politics, and that from all information at his disposal, from the general attitude and maneuvers of some individuals and groups, and from publications during the past few months, "it was clear that those who aspire to lead the nation on the return to civilian rule have not learnt any lesson from the past experiences."[84] The speech aroused hostility among politicians, students, and the press. Against a background of increasing government corruption and inefficiency, Gowon's indefinite prolongation of military politics was extremely unpopular within the nation. Thus, it was no surprise when, on 29 July 1975, the Gowon junta was toppled by a further coup. The coup plotters promised a return to a democratically elected government by 1979 and set out a clear and coherent timetable to that effect.[85]

Murtala Mohammed, the new head of state, addressed the nation and said that the events of the past few years had indicated that despite Nigeria's great human and material resources, the government had not been able to fulfil the legitimate expectation of Nigerians. He observed:

---

81. Ayandele, *Educated Elite in the Nigerian Society*, 140.
82. Ayandele, 140.
83. Ojiako, *13 Years of Military Rule*, 77.
84. Ojiako, 77.
85. Ojiako, 78.

> Nigeria has been left to drift. This situation, if not arrested, would inevitably have resulted in chaos and even bloodshed. In the endeavour to build a strong, united and virile nation, Nigerians have shed much blood. The thought of further bloodshed, for whatever reasons, must, I am sure be revolting to our people. The Armed Forces, having examined the situation came to the conclusion that certain changes were inevitable.[86]

The Mohammed junta was determined to bring about an ethical revolution in Nigerian politics. On 1 August 1979, he called for "Clean Government." He said, "This administration will not condone the misuse or misappropriation of public funds both in the Federal Government and at state levels."[87] Mohammed indeed carried out the great clean up that shook the nation – even the "untouchables" were touched in the exercise. Thus, its regime was able to prove it is neither the constitution nor the federal system of government that was at fault but merely those who operated it. The reasons given for those affected – through being dismissed, retiring, or having their appointment terminated – were poor health, doubtful integrity, redundancy, inefficiency, irresponsibility, poor attitude to work, old age, and high absence from duty without proper authority. The purge was carried out in the public sector and government-owned companies and affected both the military and civilians throughout the federation. It was hoped that the "clean-up" would cause all public office holders to put efficiency and service to the nation first.[88]

The Head of State, Murtala Mohammed, swore in the newly appointed permanent secretaries in the federal ministries. During the ceremony the thirty permanent secretaries took an oath to an ethical code of conduct in service. Each solemnly declared, swore, and pledged his or her loyalty in the service of the country.

> I will be faithful and will bear true allegiance to the Federal Republic of Nigeria at all time.
> I will never discriminate on the basic of religion, tribe, cult, or status or practice any form of partiality in the performance of my official duties.

---

86. Speech given by Murtala Muhammed on 30 July 1975 in *Fellow Country Men and Women*.

87. Ojiako, *13 Years of Military Rule*, 84.

88. Ojiako, 84–126.

> I will always place service to the public above selfish interest, realizing that a public office is a public trust.
> I will always perform my official duties diligently and efficiently, and will not engage or be involved in any activity, in conflict either directly or indirectly with this pledge.
> I will eschew and expose corruption in the performance of my official duties, and will also not corrupt others nor aid and abet corruption in all facets and outside the public service.
> I will always follow the path of justice, honesty and concord in all I do. So help me God![89]

A critical examination of the above oath of office reveals what work ethics in Nigerian politics ought to be. This military political "messiah," in his healthy revolution and political evolution, created more new states with new identities, which erased their geographical locations. New names were given, to erase memories of past political ties and emotional attachments.[90] His program of purging Nigerian politics of its "dead wood" (those that he deemed useless or unneccessary), depicted true despotism. This ethical revolution in public services was a good strategy for dealing with the most obsolete forces in governance, which had made the Gowon junta insensitive to the most sensitive moral issues of the nation. The exercise was used by privileged elements of the junta and bureaucracy to avenge themselves on opponents and challenges. Thus, the reformist genuine intentions originally designed to inject new blood and instill fresh verve into Nigerian politics was abused and became a vengeful retrenchment that brought acute pain and untold suffering to many Nigerian families.[91]

The Murtala regime initially had good democratic political intentions – a grassroots political style and program for re-civilization, which Murtala never had time to execute. The Nigerian political hero, Nwankwo, describes him thus: "The composition of the constitution drafting committee, which he appointed, as well as the despotic mannerisms inherent in the working of the transition process which he laid down, tended to suggest that Murtala Mohammed became a hero because he died before one could say '1979' was a reality."[92] On 13 February 1976, the "Nigerian Hero" was assassinated in an abortive coup and Obasanjo succeeded him. In his broadcast, Obasanjo assured the nation

---

89. Ojiako, 127.
90. Ojiako, 130–131.
91. Nwankwo, *African Dictators*, 110.
92. Nwankwo, 110.

of the continuity of Mohammed's program and that there would be no change in the policies of the federal military government.

In a frank and difficult broadcast in July 1978, Obasanjo, like the biblical Joshua, traced the event that led to military intervention in Nigerian politics in 1966, and gave harsh words on the performance of civilian politicians in the First Republic. Military intervention, according to him, was a child of circumstance:

> Circumstances of unbridled defiance and practices of democracy on the part of the political elites, their negative disposition towards the unity, and consequent peace and stability of the nation and their culpable tendency towards tribal polarization . . .[93]

The Obasanjo junta stated their willingness to return to a democratically elected government without fear or favor. He blew the whistle on the "game" of politics to begin with and warned the political leaders to learn from the lessons of the past. Political parties were registered and elections carried out which eventually ushered in the Second Republic and Alhaji Shehu Shagari as the president-elect. The political activities of the Second Republic will be discussed later under "democratic politics"; however, the first phase of military politics came to an end after thirteen years of military dictatorship.

Second Phase of Military Politics

The Mohammed-Obasanjo regime handed over the political scepter of the country to civil rule, which only lasted for four years (1979–1983). On 31 December 1983, as a result of the excesses and irresponsibility of the civilian politicians, military politicians re-entered the Nigerian political scene and stayed in power for another sixteen years with the reigns of four generals. General Buhari emerged as the new head of state. The junta under his leadership declared itself to be an offshoot of the last military administration under generals Mohammed and Obasanjo.[94] The political leadership of the Second Republic was condemned for circumventing most of the checks and balances in the 1979 constitution, and thus bringing the nation to a state of general insecurity.

General Buhari lamented that the premium on political power was so exceedingly high that political contestants regarded victory at elections as

---

93. Ojiako, *13 Years of Military Rule*, 194.
94. Ojiako, 30.

worthy of a life and death struggle, and were determined to capture or retain power by all means. Condemning the corruption and indiscipline of their civilian counterparts, he declared:

> This government will not tolerate kickbacks, inflation of contracts, and over-invoicing of imports, et cetera. Nor will it condone forgery, fraud, embezzlement, misuse and abuse of office, and illegal dealings in foreign exchange and smuggling.[95]

When Buhari's government started its purging exercise to rid Nigerian politics of corruption and indiscipline, "the list of their victims included some of the most awe-inspiring, hitherto untouchable members of the northern and other ruling elites across the board."[96] In an attempt to "salvage" the nation from ruin wrought by civilian politicians of the Second Republic, the regime used draconian decrees and computerized methods of torture to terrorize the populace.[97]

The Buhari military junta launched a moral program – "War against Indiscipline" (WAI) – which was used to control disorderly officials in public places and offices. This moral program was intended to correct impatience and disorderliness, to improve work ethics, and to stop truancy, indolence, laziness, idleness, and the like. It was also meant to improve nationalistic patriotism, that is, the national consciousness, integration, unity, and selfless services; to prevent corruption and economic sabotage; and finally, to promote environmental sanitation in homes, offices, schools, markets, hospitals, parks, and towns.

The enforcement of the "moral-WAI" deepened the national understanding of the need for a public moral consciousness for Nigerians. But as usual, WAI perished with the regime when it was overthrown in the coup of 27 August 1985, which ushered in the Babangida junta.[98] However, the intervention of another faction of military was a relief. The populace were happy to be free of their psychological, social, economic, and physical stresses.[99]

The new regime, led by the Babangida junta, played on the psychology of the people, and correctly captured the mood of the nation. It struck the right card from the very beginning. General Babangida expressed sorrow that,

---

95. "Fellow Countrymen and Women," 56.
96. Kukah, *Democracy and Civil Society in Nigeria*, 6.
97. Nwankwo, *African Dictators*, 108.
98. Dzurgba, *Nigerian Politics and Moral Behaviour*, 46.
99. Kukah, *Democracy and Civil Society in Nigeria*, 76.

> Contrary to expectations, we have so far been subjected to a steady deterioration in the general condition of living, and intolerable suffering by the ordinary Nigerian has reached unprecedented heights. Steps will be taken to ensure a comprehensive strategy of economic reforms. The innocent cannot suffer the crimes of the guilty. The guilty should be punished, only as a lesson for the future. In line with this [it is the] government's intention to uphold fundamental human rights.[100]

In order to fulfil his promise, the regime decided for the first time in Nigeria's history to ask Nigerians what they really wanted to do, especially with their economic future.[101]

In 1986, however, the Babangida junta set up a political bureau to design a political blueprint for the country. Its report was comprehensive as far as theory was concerned. But the work of intellectual theoreticians and the agenda of a military dictatorship were at variance. The Political Bureau Report made two very significant observations about the direction of Nigerian politics. The committee recommended two political parties and then suggested something those on the left took to mean a socialist government. However, the report of the experts was not a sacred document to be followed; most of the issues would have been taken care of later on. The military politicians however had other ideas. Right from the onset, military politics began to move in its own direction.[102]

The Babangida government commenced its politicking by clearing the political "deck" in Nigeria. "It sought replacement by displacement. It did this by a systematic process of elimination of those regarded as the old breed politicians and their replacement with what was called 'new breed.'"[103] Babangida registered two political parties and planned a transitional program which would claim elections in 1993. The government went on to build political party secretaries in all the local government and state capitals of the country and also took on the duty to fund the political parties for its new breed politicians. The two political parties created and sponsored were the Social Democratic Party (SDP) and the National Republican Convention (NRC); the National Electoral Commission (NEC) was set up to manage the elections. These political activities led to the famous political crisis popularly known as

---

100. Nwankwo, *African Dictators*, 108.
101. Kukah, *Democracy and Civil Society in Nigeria*, 78.
102. Kukah, 38.
103. Kukah, 80.

"June 12 crisis" (which has been recognized now as Democracy Day in honor of M. K. O. Abiola). The staggered elections were held from April to June 1993. Then, for reasons only known to the military junta, the presidential election was annulled along with the previous elections held since April.

The June 12 crisis led to widespread protests, which became particularly violent in the southwest of Nigeria. This is due to the fact that the apparent winner, M. K. O. Abiola, was from that part of the country. Again, this political crisis revitalized the existing ethnic prejudice, revelry, discrimination, and hatred. It became difficult to maintain law and order in Nigeria. As a result, coupled with external pressure, President Ibrahim Babangida "stepped aside" to Chief Ernest Shonekan, forming an Interim National Government (ING). (Both Abiola and Shonekan hailed from Abeokuta in the southwest of Nigeria.) But the dictator's manipulation could not quell the situation.

Then, another "messiah-general," Sani Abacha, stepped into the political drama, and the moral grief and darkness into which the country was thrown were evidence of a deep-seated structural deficiency which had been in the design itself. Babangida's transition program introduced new politics of economic crime into the nation. It was during this regime that hundreds of financial institutions and wonder banks sprang up in every nook and cranny of the country. Crooked accounting procedures and bad money were injected into the system and the country was faced with an economy powered by drug-laundered and fraud-ridden money in the hands of "Nigerian 419ers" that took center stage.[104]

"The government of General Sani Abacha appeared as the knight in shining armour, sacking the Shonekan-led interim government on November 17, 1994."[105] When Abacha came in, most of the key actors jumped onto the bandwagon. Some of them hoped that Abacha would install Abiola with time. But this single decision to install Abiola merely deepened the crisis of democracy by introducing many intervening variables. The politics of co-opting people into position adopted by the Abacha junta further deepened the resentment of the people, especially the Yoruba, as they believed that even though General Oladipo Diya (a Yoruba man) was the vice-president, it was a puppet position with no power.[106]

Although General Abacha was accused of being power hungry and not willing to leave the seat of power, he launched a transition program aimed at

---

104. Kukah, 82; Dzurgba, *Nigerian Politics and Moral Behaviour*, 76.
105. Kukah, 109.
106. Kukah, 109.

a democratically elected government to take over in 1997. Thus, five political parties were registered with the establishment of the National Electoral Commission of Nigeria (NECON). Between June 1997 and April 1998, staggered elections were held for all levels, except the presidential election. The five political parties agreed on Abacha as the only qualified presidential candidate. Hence, there was no need for further voting – Abacha was automatically elected president by the five political parties. The only "opposition party" organized themselves as the National Democratic Coalition (NADECO).[107] NADECO protested through the mysterious "Radio Kudirat."[108] During this regime, a wounded "lion" was let loose which resulted in a series of murders and assassinations and NADECO was alleged to be responsible. With hindsight, the Abacha transition program was geared towards his personal ambition. The nearer the transition program got to its completion, the more dangerous events surfaced their ugly heads until the final crash which caught Nigerians unawares. The danger signs became obvious even to Abacha predecessors, Buhari and Babangida, who had remained quiet all these years. They both, in different public forays, alerted the nation to the problems of corruption and the urgency for democratization.[109] The regime had no respect for human rights; it defied all appeals from all quarters. To Abacha, no human was capable of hindering his ambition to succeed and thus perpetuate his dynasty – only divine intervention could manage that.

There was jubilation all over the country at the death of Abacha on 8 June 1998.[110] The dark blanket of death had crept in to deliver democracy in Nigeria. General Abdul salami Abubaka took the mantle of leadership on 10 June 1998 as the head of state and commander-in-chief of the Armed Forces of Nigeria. As obedient citizens, Nigerians embraced the Abubaka junta unconditionally. He formed his government and launched a political transition program aimed at restoring peace, stability, and development. The junta started addressing the prevailing political issues and problems and the Abubaka administration released political prisoners. But on 8 July 1998, Nigerians heard news of the

---

107. Dzurgba, *Nigerian Politics and Moral Behaviour*, 79.

108. NADECO was made up of unidentified individuals who opposed Abacha's government. They used a radio station with an unknown location named after the late Abiola's wife (Radio Kudirat). This station was monitoring and exposing every secret action of the Abacha junta, and due to the NADECO activities, Abacha sent out some "army boys" to eliminate any suspected enemy or members of Radio Kudirat.

109. Kukah, *Democracy and Civil Society in Nigeria*, 214–215; Dzurgba, *Nigerian Politics and Moral Behaviour*, 50.

110. The government identified Abacha's cause of death as a sudden heart attack.

death on 7 July of Chief M. K. O. Abiola, the pillar and cornerstone of the entire democratic struggle in the Nigerian political scene, since the 12 June crisis. The sad event occurred at a most crucial time when Abiola was about to be released by the military government so that Nigeria could genuinely move on to greatness. Most Nigerians saw this as foul play by the junta politicians. Kukah writes:

> The circumstances of the Chief's death in the presence of the United States Assistant Secretary of State for African Affairs, Mr. Thomas Pickering, and his delegation from Washington, remain inexplicable. If as Nigerians believed, God had saved them from General Abacha, the death of Chief Abiola himself, tragic as it was, was indeed another sign of the finger of God in Nigeria's affairs. Nigerians skating on very thin political ice believed that God resolved their problems for them by direct intervention. This thinking gained currency precisely because of the emotions among those who believed that the death of General Abacha meant the ascension to power of Chief Abiola.[111]

Kukah further concludes that Nigerians should ponder and think about the circumstances that surrounded the death of these great political leaders in Nigerian political scenarios so we can appreciate and know that truly God saved them from pending anarchy. However, the death of Abacha and Abiola turned a new leaf in Nigerian politics. Could it be that the two "political heros" were sacrificed for Nigerian democracy to move forward?

The Abubaka military junta felt that Nigeria must move forward, thus the government launched a transition program as follows:

1. Local government elections, 5 December 1998.
2. State governorship and assembly elections, 9 January 1999.
3. National assembly elections, 20 February 1999.
4. Presidential elections, 27 February 1999.
5. Presidential swearing-in, 29 May 1999.[112]

The government also established the Independent National Electoral Commission (INEC) and three political parties were registered: Peoples Democratic Party (PDP), All Peoples Party (APP), and Alliance for Democracy (AD). The various elections were held with little adjustment according to the

---
111. Kukah, *Democracy and Civil Society in Nigeria*, 297–298.
112. Kukah, 297–298.

formal schedule and Chief Olusegun Obasanjo (PDP) was the winner of the presidential election against Chief Olu Falae (APP/AD). The elections were assessed as free, fair, and peaceful – there were a few malpractices here and there, but they were too insignificant to nullify the authenticity and validity of the election results.

Indeed, on 29 May 1999, President Obasanjo was inaugurated as the President of the Federal Republic of Nigeria. Thus Nigeria was set free from the neo-independence junta politics, a politics of military dictatorship. Even though military politicians always claimed that they had come to wage war against corruption and indiscipline, they left the Nigerian political scene even worse off than the moral diseases they supposedly came to cure. In fact, the military junta only displayed self-aggrandizement. Without personal integrity with the fear of God, no regime, even under democracy as the next chapter will disclose, can genuinely instill discipline in the conduct of the national political affairs.

4

New Era of Democratic Politics in Nigeria

In Nigeria, even though independence-era democracies and democrats have been overthrown, ridiculed, banished, and tortured, the national aspiration for democratic politics has refused to die. Elected rulers quashed and jailed the opposition and mocked democracy in the midst of their own self-aggrandizement. Military hegemony swept away discredited electoral politics and civilian governments that challenged the established order. But invariably, national pressure for a democratic political representative government reasserted itself.[1] The first occurred from 1979 to 1983, which was later crushed and surfaced again in 1999 to the present. This democratic renaissance has been a credit to Nigeria, which has long been viewed as a kind of model and testing ground for the rest of the African nations.

It was with great expectation and much fanfare that in 1999 the Nigerian military politicians returned power to the civilian-elected government after twenty-nine years of military dictatorship out of her forty-four years of independence.[2] The discussion will be in three sections as follows: (1) the inter-testament democratic politics in Nigeria, which is the Second Republic; (2) the New Era democracy in Nigerian politics, which commenced with the Obasanjo civilian regime; and (3) moral issues arising from the nascent democracy.

Inter-Testament Democratic Politics in Nigeria

On 1 October 1979, the Nigerian military junta once again had a democratically elected government freely chosen by voters from a range of competing people

---
1. Diamond, *Class, Ethnicity and Democracy in Nigeria*.
2. Kukah, *Democracy and Civil Society in Nigeria*, 6–10.

running. This occurred after "thirteen years of military rule, a ghastly civil war, and one of the most imaginative and carefully designed transitions ever staged by a withdrawing military government."[3] Unlike the Gowon junta politics, which procrastinated on the issues of democratic politics and state-creation, the Murtala-Obasanjo junta politics saw the prompt resolution of state issues, and the disengagement of the military politicians, as essential to its image and legitimacy as a corrective government.[4]

On the eve of the Second Republic, five fresh, new parties came into existence and were officially recognized by national commissions designated by the Federal Electoral Commission (FEDECO). These parties were: the Great Nigerian Peoples Party (GNPP), the National Party of Nigeria (NPN), the Nigerian Peoples Party (NPP), the Peoples Redemption Party (PRP), and the Unity Party of Nigeria (UPN). This new trend of political parties competed in elections nationally during the inter-testament period of military governance in Nigeria. Their successes varied with each election – elections to the House of Representatives and the Senate. The leaders or presidential aspirants of the five parties were Ibrahim Waziri (GNPP), Shehu Shagari (NPN), Nnamdi Azikiwe (NPP), Aminu Kano (PRP), and Obafemi Awolowo (UPN).[5]

Among these five political leaders, Shehu Shagari became the first elected president of Nigeria! Thus a new system of civilian government was inaugurated – an executive presidential system. It was indeed a new but more complicated democratic government that required the patience and a new moral attitude and behavior of Nigerians – civilians and military alike. Unfortunately, those leading the new democratic government appeared not ready to learn from the past experiences. The governed as well, including the military, were impatient, not allowing time to understand the implications of the new political development. To crown it all, the first civilian-conducted election after the military politicians had left political power was badly implemented. Rigging was the order of the day in the 1983 election. As a result of these moral misconducts, the military made a second return to capture political power in Nigeria in a bloodless coup.[6]

The inter-testament democracy was overthrown on 30 December 1983 by the Buhari junta government. One interesting aspect of the 1979–1983 democratic period was the moral program initiated by Shagari called the

---

3. Dzurgba, *Nigerian Politics and Moral Behaviour*, 46.

4. Dzurgba, 46.

5. Oyediran, *Introduction to Political Science*, 58.

6. Oyediran, 88, 90.

"Ethical Revolution." Revolution means a great and complete change in conditions and ways of doing things, morally and otherwise. The Ethical Revolution was an extremely important national objective and well-intended program of moral orientation.[7] It was an important achievement of the Shagari government (even though there was little or no effect upon the people), because it drew Nigerians' attention, for the first time since Nigerian independence, to the imperative demand of moral consciousness and behavior in a search for a democratic political process. It emphasized the need for political ethics in Nigerian politics. This is why this book is relevant, because until now Nigeria has not experienced an ethical revolution. Rather, what we are seeing in our national democracy is a decline or lack of moral integrity.

Nigerian wealth and power are unevenly distributed among the citizens. Many Nigerians struggle to earn a daily living, having little or no material possessions and probably no hope of improving their lot. In the midst of abject poverty, Nigerian politicians and their entourages "often accumulate and flaunt massive wealth, which to a degree is expected and accepted in Nigerian society."[8] The majority of these politicians are always in power because of their network of patronage; these elite receive political support as they secure and distribute labor. "The system allows for some redistribution of income because patrons often pay for things such as school fees and marriage costs for relatives, community development, and charity work."[9]

This unequal distribution of wealth has a severe effect on children's health. One-fifth of Nigerian children die before the age of five from treatable diseases such as pneumonia, whooping cough, malaria, diarrhea, and measles. A good number of infants are not immunized against measles and many of the children under the age of five are affected by malnutrition. Some adults are also affected, although with less resulting deaths. According to Stock, "Only 20% of rural Nigerians and 52% of urban Nigerians have access to safe water. One-third has no access to health care simply because they live too far from clinics or other treatment centres. Many others cannot afford the fees charged by clinics."[10]

Many urban Nigerians are not finding life easy either. Poverty in the city is as pervasive as poverty in the village, although average incomes are higher and death rates lower in urban areas compared to rural areas. "All ingredients

---

7. Dzurgba, *Nigerian Politics and Moral Behaviour*, 46.
8. Robert Stock, "Nigeria," Microsoft® Encarta® 2009 [DVD]. Redmond, WA: Microsoft Corporation, 2008.
9. Stock.
10. Stock.

of better life need money and many are lured to the city in hope of receiving a regular income. A better education further attracts people to leave their rural districts."[11] Unfortunately, "secure, well-paying jobs are scarce, even for those with considerable education." Food is very expensive in cities; housing is costly as well; sewage disposal systems in most Nigerian towns are poorly constructed; and contaminated wells, streams, roadside drains and other bodies of water escalate the possibility of contacting infectious disease. The burning of wood for fuel and automobile industries "further pollute the air and water."[12]

Robert Stock opines that due to a high rate of unemployment, poor economic and social inequality, there were increases in crime, especially in mid-1990s, coupled with incompetency and corruption of the Nigerian police and customs forces. There are more cases of thefts, burglaries, and break-ins as well as armed robberies, just to mention a few. Stock stresses further that,

> Nigeria is a major conduit for drugs moving from Asia and Latin America to markets in Europe and North America. Large-scale Nigerian fraud rings have targeted business people in other parts of the world. The business people are invited to help transfer large sums of money out of Nigeria, with the promise of a share of the transferred money. Advance fees are requested to expedite this transfer, but the advanced money routinely disappears. Although there have been periodic campaigns to root out corrupt politicians and attack crime, they have had little lasting effect.[13]

More so, in the 1990s there were many cases of periodic violent clashes among different ethnic groups and religious fanatics. Most of these clashes were a result of local political disputes and land conflicts as well as Muslim and Christian disputes. Many politicians and religious leaders have manipulated these crises for their selfish interest. This was the social-political situation when Obasanjo came into power as civilian president on 29 May 1999.

New Era of Democracy in Nigerian Politics

Nigerian politics are both passionate and acrimonious in nature. For a period of time, democratic stability, national integration, sustainable socio-economic development, and moral sanity have eluded Nigerian post-colonial

---

11. Hans Haselbarth, *Christian Ethics in the African Context*, 110.
12. Stock, "Nigeria," Microsoft® Encarta.
13. Stock.

politics. Although the state attained formal political independence from British hegemony on 1 October 1960, Nigeria still remains one of the most underdeveloped post-colonial nations in the world. The nation is characterized by high external debt, inflation, poverty, malnutrition, institutional decay in health, education and general infrastructures, urban dislocation, and violent crimes.[14] However, this section will make a brief survey of the political and moral issues that took place in the nascent democracy of the Obasanjo administration.

29 May 1999, marked the end of military politics in Nigeria when the Third Republic was ushered in. (This is taking into account the First Republic of Abukakar Tafawa Balewa,1960–1966, and the Second Republic of Shehu Shagari, 1979–1983.) Following the Second Nigerian Republic there were the military regimes of Mohammed Buhari (1983–1985), Ibrahim Babangida (1985–1993), Sani Abacha (1993–1998) and Abdul salami Abubaka (1998–1999). The new era of democracy commenced with Olusegun Obasanjo (1999–2007), Umaru Yar'Adua (2007–2010), Goodluck Jonathan (2007–2015), and Muhammadu Buhari (2015–), who is serving as President of Nigeria (at the time of publication of this book). However, the moral assessment of the new era is limited to Obasanjo administration from 1999 to 2004, which marked the new beginning of democracy in Nigeria. This research was carried out when Olusegun Obasanjo was the incumbent president.

Nevertheless, 1999 was "the last bus stop" of twenty-nine years of military dictatorship in Nigerian politics and the adoption of a new constitution. In this constitution, "Nigeria is a federal republic with a democratically elected government made of separate executive, legislative, and judicial branches."[15] The new document guarantees Nigerians full human rights: the rights to life, liberty, and security of Nigerians; freedom from military torture or cruel punishment from anybody; and the right to legal representation and a fair trial or to equal treatment before any court in Nigeria. It also includes freedom of movement and residence in any part of the nation; freedom of religion, thought, conscience and opinion as citizens of Nigeria; freedom of expression in speech or in writing; the right of peaceful gathering; the right to take part in the governance of Nigeria; and to equal access to public services without any form of discrimination based on place of origin or ethnicity, sex or religion.[16]

The Federal Republic of Nigeria is the official name of the nation with a federal form of government; it consists of thirty-six states and a federal capital

---

14. Abubakar, "Federal Character Principle," 164.
15. Stock, "Nigeria," Microsoft® Encarta.
16. See Stott, *Issues Facing Christians Today*, 193.

territory, Abuja, which is a city in a scenic valley of rolling grassland located in the center of the nation. "A large hill known as Aso Rock provides the backdrop for the city's government district, which is laid out along three axes representing the executive, legislative, and judicial branches . . . Abuja has an international airport and is linked to other cities in Nigeria by a network of highways."[17]

Olusegun Obasanjo was born in 1935, and became a two-time leader of Nigeria, first as a military head of state (1976–1979) and then as the country's first civilian president since 1983 when he took office for the second time (1999–2007). Obasanjo was born in Abeokuta, a city in southwestern Nigeria. "Unable to afford a university education, he joined the Nigerian military in 1958 and received training in the United Kingdom and India."[18] He succeeded Brigadier Murtala Ramat Muhammed as Nigeria's military leader when Muhammed was assassinated in 1976. Obasanjo followed through with Muhammed's plan to return Nigeria to civilian rule in 1979, becoming the first of Nigeria's ruling generals to voluntarily surrender power to a civilian government. The decision to step aside won him international praise. "He retired from the military following the 1979 handover. He ran a chicken farm and worked on a variety of international projects with the United Nations (UN) and other groups. This work raised Obasanjo's international profile and at one time he was considered for the job of UN secretary general."[19] Obasanjo also strengthened his relationships with international leaders such as former US president Jimmy Carter, whom he had befriended while in power. Obasanjo became a vocal critic of the Abacha regime, and in 1995 he was imprisoned on charges that he had plotted a coup against Abacha. He was released from prison after Abacha's death in June 1998.

Major General Abdulsalam Abubakar succeeded Abacha, and in August 1998 Abubakar announced plans to hand power to a civilian government in May 1999. Obasanjo initially declared he would not run for president, but he later changed his mind due to the influence of Rev Prof Yusuf Ameh Obaje (who later become the Aso Rock Chaplain), and he ran as the candidate of the military-civilian PDP. In campaigning, Obasanjo cast himself as the only candidate capable of providing a bridge between military and civilian rule, but many Nigerians were wary of electing someone with close ties to the military. After taking office, Obasanjo worked to overcome the distrust resulting from

---

17. "Abuja," Microsoft® Encarta® 2009 [DVD]. Redmond, WA: Microsoft Corporation, 2008.

18. "Olusegun Obasanjo," Microsoft® Encarta® 2009 [DVD]. Redmond, WA: Microsoft Corporation, 2008.

19. "Olusegun Obasanjo.

his military background. He overhauled corrupt governmental systems, improved the economy, and guarded against ethnic divisions. However, widespread clashes between religious and ethnic groups, killing thousands of Nigerians, plagued Obasanjo's first years in office. Even so, he was re-elected in April 2003.[20]

Nevertheless, this democracy was a major change in the political history of Nigeria. It marked the beginning of a new era in Nigerian democratic politics. The military politicians lasted for sixteen years. The nature of any military administration is authoritarian and totalitarian, abusing political power. It is a coercive governance, which demands a compulsive obedience and loyalty. Its precision in governing leaves no room for questioning, debate, and dialogue.[21] These military principles of behavior gave the military administration in Nigeria an image of totalitarianism and dictatorship. This is the political ideology which civilian politicians inherited in thought, action, and behavior. Therefore, a change from this totalitarian orientation, which dominated Nigerian politics, to a civilian-political orientation, is a difficult process requiring a moral assessment, and time, patience, understanding, and tolerance. This is the background to the third republican civilian governance of the Nigerian Republic.[22]

The transition from military politics to democratic politics brought into being political institutions which included the INEC, political parties, local government councils, state assemblies, the national assembly, and the executive. These political institutions have been sustained in spite of the initial fears and threats. Compared to the military regime, there was a greater recognition of fundamental rights and freedoms. Nigerians started to express their freedom of opinion, conscience, and religion without fear. Freedom of press is guaranteed as well. The mass media now broadcasts news and publishes information with little or no censorship and restrictions. In this context, the courts and the police have been liberated to exercise their duties and powers without fear and threats of being harassed by government security agents. It is in this direction that the rule of law, which is no respecter of persons, will develop to an appreciable level in the judiciary. This is what is known as the equality of men and women before the law.[23]

---

20. "Olusegun Obasanjo."
21. Dzurgba, *Nigeria Politics and Moral Behaviour*, 101.
22. Dzurgba, 101.
23. Dzurgba, 101.

The Obasanjo administration set up the Justice Chukwudifu Oputa Commission and inaugurated the panel to investigate the grievances individuals and social groups had against one another, which had resulted from the previous military regimes in particular. The Oputa Commission intended to investigate and establish the causes and the implications of past and present grievances that existed in the public service, private sector, and armed forces. The move was an unprecedented searchlight for the entire country. The aim of the Oputa commission was to work towards the reconciliation of affected Nigerians. Mutual understanding, tolerance, and accommodation were sought for through the commission. It was hoped and anticipated that the proper understanding of nationwide grievances would facilitate the healing of deep-seated and heart-breaking old wounds in Nigerian politics. Dzurgba writes:

> It was hoped that the anticipated healing could lead to social and political well being in Nigeria. Justice Oputa commission made grave and surprising revelations which brought the Nigerian public to a reasonable understanding of the past immoral and criminal intrigues, manipulations, maneuvers, plots, conspiracies and hatches in both low and high places in the Nigerian society.[24]

In other words, these disclosures have increased the awareness of immoral and criminal behavior in Nigerian politics. The government believes that this will encourage patriotic Nigerians to work towards decent political behavior.

In the first few months of the junta government under review, there was a series of impeachments. The senate president at the time was impeached on forgery and perjury in relation to a law degree qualification from the UK. In the same vein, the speaker of the House of Representatives was impeached for forgery and perjury in relation to a degree in business administration obtained from the University of Toronto in Canada. And the senate president was also impeached on the grounds of mismanagement of funds. None of these impeached leaders reacted negatively; rather they accepted the judgment of the National Assembly. These politicians demonstrated political maturity and humility. These impeachments yielded democratic virtues and encouraged a peaceful resolution of other political crises during the Obasanjo administration.[25]

There were a series of dividends of democracy in this new era of politics in Nigeria under the Obasanjo Administration. The role of the non-governmental

---

24. Dzurgba, 102.
25. Dzurgba, 103.

organizations (NGOs) which had existed during the military eras received a boost and proper recognition, while new ones came into existence. For instance, the wife of the president, Stella Obasanjo, established the Child Care Trust (CCT), an NGO whose branches spread across the country. The CCT provides welfare services for all classes of children and also tackles the problems associated with child abuse. Another NGO, the Women Trafficking and Child Labour Eradication Foundation (WOTCLEF), was established by the wife of the vice-president, Titi Amina Atiku-Abubakar. This NGO fights for the abolition and prevention of the kidnapping of women and children who are taken to foreign countries for monetary gains. These and other NGOs form a part of what is politically known as "civil society."

In order to fight against corrupt practices and related offences in the public and private sectors of Nigerian society, the Obasanjo government established the Independent Corrupt Practices Commission (ICPC). The main objective of the ICPC was to assist the government in the effort to reduce, and perhaps eradicate, corruption in society. In taking a critical look at the political history of Nigeria, one will observe a kind of national integration as a result of political corruption. Partnership in corruption seems to have helped Nigerian politicians, both military and civilian, to overcome the old regional, ethnic, and religious barriers to political stability, thus overcoming the divisions that could have resulted in destructive conflicts. One will agree with Olatunji who cited Nego's observation:

> Many retired and serving armed forces men and civilians are now millionaires. Some of them have multi-million Naira agricultural farms, shipping firms, airline companies, big contracting firms, etc. On the part of the non-elite, corruption has helped to reduce the gap between government officials and the illiterate farmers who come around to welcome him with traditional gifts.[26]

This is the kind of development that corruption has brought into Nigerian politics. In the political arena today we see military and civilian upper classes, whether retired or in service, coming together to maintain the already existing political culture. Thus, in the midst of multi-billionaires, we are witnessing a democratic era of austerity with plunging oil revenues, massive unemployment, a worthless currency, abject poverty, colossal national debt, and a lot of other socio-political and economic problems. How long will Nigeria continue in this political mess?

---

26. Olatunji, "Public, Accountability and Nation Building," 90.

When the Obasanjo-civilian administration came to power with its moral campaign and programs, hopes were raised that bribery and its twin sister, corruption, would be nailed to the cross. Amazingly though, the stories remained the same. What actually is wrong? What gave birth to this moral decadence in the country? What has caused this decline of integrity in Nigerian politics? These and many more questions will be answered in the rest of this book, while the next segment of this chapter will assess the place of moral integrity in Nigerian politics.

Moral Issues in the Nascent Democratic Politics

The democratic politics of this Third Republic have witnessed unprecedented political assassinations – more than all the previous civilian and military governments in Nigeria since 1 October 1960. Nigeria has lost prominent men and women who were murdered in cold blood across the country in the name of politics. Prominent among them are Chief Bola Ige, a serving attorney-general and minister of justice; Chief Dikibo, PDP vice-chairman of the South-South political zone; Chief Akiga of Benue state, and others. The insecurity of life and property are a major crisis in the Nigerian political scene.

In 1999, a military intervention in the village of Odi in Bayelsa State led to the killing and injuring of some soldiers who were on a mission of intervention. As a result of the killings, the soldiers who ought to have protected life and property overreacted and razed the village. The degree of violence inflicted on the community went beyond normal military intervention in a civil crisis situation. In the same vein, in Tiv-Jukun in 2000, there was mismanagement and application of military violence in Tiv land. The soldiers rampaged and razed six villages, and innocent civilians were killed in cold blood. Some soldiers also went to the home village of the former chief-of-army staff, General Victor Malu, razed his house, and killed his uncle with his two wives. It was a clear case of the purposeful abuse of military power in the name of democracy. Dzurgba opined that this ugly phenomenon may be attributed to the long period of years of militarization in the enculturation of the Nigeria civilians. Practical democratic politics has been forgotten for many years and Nigerians are used to military intervention in political matters.[27]

The Nigerians are a loving people, and Nigeria is the giant of Africa with its diverse tribes, and religious and cultural affinities, but they have forgotten issues like party formation, party affiliation, campaign hustling, voting

---

27. Dzurgba, *Nigerian Politics and Moral Behaviour*, 101.

behavior, diplomatic lobbying, healthy competition, and acceptance of defeat as an alternative to victory in practical politics. Thus, in giving democratic politics a third chance in Nigeria, Nigerians found integrity in democratic practice cumbersome and unacceptable. Nigerian politicians, therefore, pushed aside political codes of ethics and threw away an effort to acquire political offices through a democratic process. Political goodwill, mutual understanding, tolerance, godly fear, and honesty were also unacceptable to most politicians. As a result, opponents or rivals are seen as intolerable enemies who must be eliminated at all cost.[28]

Most Nigerian politicians have bought into the moral idea of Thrasymachus, an ancient Greek philosopher, who believed that "justice is the interest of the stronger party." That is to say, what is morally right is defined by the one in power. Often this is understood as political power, as in the case of Machiavelli, though it could mean physical, psychological, or other kinds of power. Thus, Nigerians fail to note the difference between *power* and *goodness*. It is possible to be powerful without being good, and it is possible to be good without being powerful.[29] The former is the case in the Nigerian political scene.

Abusive language is another common yet serious moral issue in the Nigerian political scene – adversarial language is an accepted norm. Political communication today is full of curses, oaths, and the obscene. Obscene language is a verbal expression that is morally disgusting, foul, wicked, lustful, and offensive to decency, and is likely to corrupt a person.[30] In Nigerian politics, politicians and their followers lack integrity in political communication. We see situations in which politicians say severe and unjust things to, or about, their opponents.

Abusive political language is made by a politician who is driven by jealousy and hatred. This abusive language is done either in speaking or in writing. The objective of this is to release jealous, hateful, and hostile feelings, and it is calculated to expose a fellow politician whom one hates so that he or she can be seen as someone who deserves contempt, hatred, torture, or death. Dzurgba rightly points out that "abusive language makes our political language a drab language, a dull, uninterested and monotonous language. In an abusive language, inappropriate words are carefully selected for the purposes of making speeches and writing pamphlets."[31]

---

28. Dzurgba, 101.
29. Geisler, *Christian Ethics*, 17–18.
30. Dzurgba, *Nigerian Politics and Moral Behaviour*, 58.
31. Dzurgba, 58.

In other words, abusive language makes Nigerian politics metaphorically a "battlefield" in which aggression and brutality are expected. A political opponent or opposition party is seen not only as an enemy, but also as a wolf or a tiger, and this instigates physical violence. When there is violence, there is need for physical power, which requires political thugs. Thus, in such a context, integrity is at peril and in serious political danger.

Democratic politics is understood today by most Nigerians as the freedom to say whatever one wishes, whether good or bad without moral guides.[32] That is why politics in Nigeria is almost synonymous with contention and the disturbance of public order and peace. Politics becomes a distasteful and anti-social activity, which necessarily requires bad manners. Thus, Nigerian politicians and their disciples are expected to be noisy and rude in speech and behavior. In their abusive language, there is a self-evident arrogance characterized by too much pride in themselves, with too little regard for their opponents, or even the society they claim to govern. "It is in this sense that dishonesty, lies, deception and half-truths are made prominent in politics."[33] That is to say, the individual has no responsibility and accountability for his or her good public image; that the tarnishing of his or her public integrity is meaningless, lying is advantageous and deceit is overwhelming irrespective of the risks involved.

Nigerian politicians know the power of communication and love to talk to public audiences. But their communication is not to inform, teach, or persuade, rather it is to ridicule, insult, tarnish, and defame their political opponents and opposition parties. In most cases, their language is aimed at making irrelevant ideas and unprofitable programs seem bright and attractive in order to inflate the politicians' fame, to gain more favor against their opponents, or simply for public deception. Their public deception is best explained by Dzurgba:

> These politicians are usually not humble people; that they feel compelled to announce their complete rightness and that of their parties on all possible occasions. Their opponents and critics commit blunders (thoughtlessly foolish mistakes) in their interpretations, assessments and judgments. Their opponents and critics are fond of diabolical plots against humankind in general and the electorate in particular.[34]

---

32. Yamsat, *Role of the Church in Democratic Governance*, 12.
33. Yamsat, 56.
34. Dzurgba, *Nigerian Politics and Moral Behaviour*, 59.

Unfortunately, these same politicians should be the national light bearers, laboring patriotically and ceaselessly to show Nigerians how to do good politics. The fact that they should display the path that leads to peace, stability, security, and good government, makes them role models with supposedly the right political thoughts, behaviors, decisions, and actions.[35] It is understandable then why Nigerians experience moral failure in politics.

Adversarial politics in Nigerian democracy means essentially finding fault with everything the political opponents do, but exonerating everything one's own party does. If a politician belongs to a particular party, all the members of that party are good, intelligent, disciplined, and responsible, while those who belong to a different party are dishonest, deceitful, hypocritical, cunning, and stupid. The opponent members are blind to the sufferings, afflictions, and miseries of the common people, the masses. They are the ones who are saboteurs, whose desire is often to commit felonious treason against their country, their "motherland" and their "fatherland." This is how political bickering, especially in irrelevant and insignificant issues, continues to plague the politics of the nation. Infantile beliefs, ideas, and actions become self-evident among politicians and their followers, who find dignity and glory in being used as thugs, vandals, or hooligans. These political disciples are the militant loyalists who translate a heavy "verbal battle" into a physical and bloody battle in Nigerian democratic politics.[36]

Most Nigerian politicians put aside all morals and participate in violent behavior, noisy quarrels, and sword-wielding language. In such an atmosphere, these people believe in "power before usual integrity" and "political office before competence." The opponent's minor faults are exaggerated and factual information is wrongly presented. A campaign for any political office may attract a great deal of mudslinging, blackmailing, and character assassination. There can be such a complete character assassination that the men and women who are voted into public offices may have lost the integrity, trust, and confidence of those who have put them there. In the political scene, almost everyone calls each other a liar, a thief, and a fraud. The most serious thing is that the continuity of these moral vices in politics will make it increasingly difficult for decent men and women of integrity to seek public offices.[37] How long will the prudent men and women keep silent while unrighteousness pervades the national polity?

---

35. Dzurgba, 60.
36. Dzurgba, 60.
37. Dzurgba, 60.

Basically, as Kukah rightly observes, the quest for blind, naked power, and the drive towards a primitive accumulation of wealth and property, are the driving forces for politics in Nigeria. That is why politics is seen as an end game, a humanistic teleological ethics.[38] This misconception of politics and its lack of integrity has led to the emergence of professional assassins and salaried thugs and arsonists. It is in this context that the massive political corruption and misconduct, electoral malpractices, and Anambra political debacle, for instance, in which policemen abducted Anambra State governor, Dr. Chris Ngige, can be explained and understood.

The nature of moral issues arising in relationship between politics and integrity in Nigeria are obvious in the Anambra State political crisis.[39] To display the moral bankruptcy and disunity of Nigerian politicians and political leaders, the ruling party at the time, the PDP treated this touchy national issue, as well as others, as a party affair.

The political friction in Anambra State, especially between Ngige and his "political father," Uba, caused an intra-party rumpus. The Anambra crisis became a fracas between President Obasanjo and the PDP national chairman, Audu Ogbeh – the party's top leaders. This displayed a lack of integrity even within the ruling party. Most of the PDP governors believed that Ngige was a victim of an incorrect application of harsh federal economic reforms. In other words, there is a degree of indignation among the PDP members on certain actions and policies of the president.[40] This intra-party ruckus put PDP's integrity at stake before the general public.

The chairman of the ruling PDP, who alleged that the president did not do enough to curb the criminals who were holding Anambra State hostage, fired back, revealing that the two contestants in the Anambra political drama were an indication that the ruling party did not win the 2003 governorship elections. The opposition parties, especially the AD and All Nation Progressive Party (ANPP), joined the fray, calling the ruling party "a dangerous leviathan that poses a serious danger to Nigerian democracy."[41] The opposition parties were united in believing that since the PDP realized its criminality, it should surrender what it stole from the people of Anambra State.[42]

---

38. Kukah, *Democracy and Civil Society in Nigeria*, 4.
39. Dzurgba, *Nigerian Politics and Moral Behaviour*, 93.
40. Adeyemo, "Loud Family Quarrel," 16–23.
41. Babarinsa, "Unusual Gladiators," 5.
42. Babarinsa, 5.

The Anambra crisis is not an isolated problem in Nigerian politics. Each state has its own peculiar political crises just like that of Anambra State. Almost all the thirty-six states in Nigeria go through one political crisis after another, and each state's problem is bigger than that state alone. The Anambra crisis involved more than Anambra; the people there could not solve it on their own. According to Omo Omoruyi, the Anambra crisis "has to be solved through a proper dialogue among Igbo leaders as to their position in Nigeria, and their position in State, as to their position after the civil war."[43] Something is basically wrong with the moral value system in the politics of Nigeria that brings about this enormous lack of political integrity. The conflict in Anambra State revealed a great deal of political manipulations, intrigues, conspiracy, and plots which arose from a moral bankruptcy in the politics of Nigeria. It is clear that Nigerian politicians lack the appropriate ethical or moral behavior needed for political goodwill, mutual understanding, and tolerance. There seems to be no law, order, peace, sanity, or discipline.[44] Hence, the result is a colossal lack of integrity, which demands a vigorous new moral orientation in Nigerian politics.

---

43. Ero, "Presidency," 18–19. This is an interview Ero had with Omo Omoniyi.
44. Dzurgba, *Nigerian Politics and Moral Behaviour*, 109.

5

Moral Bankruptcy in Nigerian Politics

The nascent democratic political experiment in Nigeria is morally bankrupt. The happenings in the state have demonstrated that the federal government led by President Olusegun Obasanjo and the Peoples Democratic Party (PDP) has learned no lessons from the past and is setting the scene for a re-enactment of the tragedies of the past Nigerian political history. The government seems perversely determined to repeat or allow all the errors and social evils that brought the country to the brink of ruin. Nigerians thought that the installation of a retired post-military civilian president is the right person to bring the country to the democratic new order for which Nigerians yearned. But the first four years of this administration proved a great disappointment. Nigerians expected the new democratic government to attempt to restore morale, to properly restructure the Nigerian political system. This chapter assesses the causes and effects of the moral bankruptcy in the nascent Nigerian political affairs.

Causes of Moral Bankruptcy in Nigerian Politics

Many factors have contributed to the moral bankruptcy in Nigerian politics. The attempt in this section is to examine some causes that jeopardized integrity in political activities. This will throw further light as to why many Nigerians have become disillusioned with the lack of integrity in today's politics. The attitudes of most politicians and their followers have little or no room for integrity. The political culture says, "The end justifies the means." In other words, "Do or say what it takes to get what you want." Indeed, often the unscrupulous come out on top while those with integrity appear to end up at the bottom.¹ The question is, what are the causes of moral bankruptcy in Nigeria's political activities? They are many, but only a few will be discussed.

Poor Understanding of Politics and Democracy

Many Nigerians have a poor or negative concept of what politics and democracy are all about. Some people express their concept of politics in metaphoric forms, for instance, some see politics as *food*.² In other words, some people go into politics in order to get access to the shares of the "national cake." This is what Dzurgba called the "chop-chop" concept of politics³ – a concept based on a style of living with a colonial origin. This style of living is supported with necessary office allowances, which help to set politicians apart from the rest of Nigerians. In this way, Nigerian politicians and public officers arrogate to themselves an honorable lifestyle and prefer to stay in the Government Reservation Area (GRA) owning big, expensive cars in order to attract much respect from the general public.

In the midst of abject poverty, these "privilege politicians" live extravagant lives which only a few of them can finance honestly, along with other perks such as the provision of food, clothing, health, education, and transport fares.⁴ This extravagance leads to all kinds of moral vices and maneuvering to defraud government funds meant for public development. This conspicuous consumption does not encourage self-discipline, self-control, independence, or self-respect. It does not encourage hard work, diligence, dedication, productivity and accountability.⁵ Rather, it promotes a rush for the acquisition of power and wealth at all costs.

There are those who also see politics as a *war*. With this mentality, political opponents are seen as enemies who do not deserve to live.⁶ Thus, the day of election is a day of battle and indeed party members are armed and ready to crush anybody that will challenge their actions.⁷ On election days, voters are afraid to go out to vote. On several occasions many Nigerians who went to vote did not return. Because politics is viewed in terms of war, it

---

1. Murphy and Murphy, *International Minister's Manual*, 65.
2. Dzurgba, *Nigerian Politics and Moral Behaviour*, 54.
3. Dzurgbe, 54.
4. Dzurgba, 54.
5. Dzurgba, 54.
6. Dzurgba, 54.
7. Dzurgba, 55.

has been militarized so that hostility, aggression, and violence have become normal aspects of politics. Many politicians believe that moral vices cannot be avoided in politics.[8] They see moral vices as part and parcel of politics. It means politicians can use any means necessary to do away with a political opponent or rival. Those who see politics as war do not accept defeat.[9] And an unwillingness to accept political defeat leads to intolerance and aggression. Thus the noble aspects of political values and integrity are pushed aside in order to win by all means.

Nigerians are lacking in their understanding of democracy. Democracy is popularly understood as "the government of the people by the people for the people." Aristotle, who was a strong advocate of political democracy, said it is "the rule of the teaming poor citizens of a nation."[10] In other words, a democratic nation is the one where the poor, who are usually in the majority, have sovereign control of the government. It is the system of governing a country, recognizing the participation of the people of that country in their own governance, rather than it being the sole responsibility of the people in power.

Democracy emphasizes the freedom of the people to vote, to stand for election, and to contribute their share in the running of the government. But to most Nigerian politicians, democracy is the freedom to do as one wishes, good or bad, right or wrong, correct or incorrect, as far as they have the power and money to do and undo.[11] It is seen as a governing system where the majority vote has it all at the expense of the minority vote; this poor concept causes moral bankruptcy in politics.[12] Thus the wrong concept of political democracy among Nigerians has contributed immensely to moral vices in politics.

Lack of Ideological Basis for Party Formation

Political party formation in Nigeria lacks ideology. Ideology is a body of ideas, which prescribes a particular manner of thinking to its followers or members. It is a worldview, which provides a rationale for an existing state of society. It secures the legitimacy and the rightness of that state of society. Ideology in a

---

8. Dzurgba, 55.
9. Dzurgba, 55.
10. Dzurgba, 14.
11. Dzurgba, 57.
12. Dzurgba, 58.

political party articulates a set of ideals, goals, and methods for satisfying the needs of all its members as well as society in general.

An ideology interprets the past, explains the present, and forecasts the future. It provides a pattern of beliefs and a set of convictions, which prescribe a specific manner of reasoning, moral behavioral style, unique identity, and sound orientation in political affairs. Ideology in party formation stipulates, reconciles, and unifies the perceptions, opinions, and interests of all members in agreement with the society.[13] But taking a close look at the political parties in Nigeria, one discovers that these ideological bases are lacking.

Instead what we have is lack of continuity in party formation and inability to manifest permanent organization at the local level. In other words, Nigerian political party formation has suffered retrogression. We have a poor concept of party formation. Nigerians are intoxicated with political power. "The premium on political power is so high that we are prone to take the most extreme measures to win and to maintain political power."[14] This has contributed to moral laxity in Nigerian politics.

According to A. D. Aina, modern political parties ought to meet four criteria: (1) continuity, that is, a life span beyond those of its founder; (2) nationwide organization; (3) the desire to exercise power; and (4) consistent efforts to garner significant popular support. But the sole desire of Nigerian parties is the exercise of political power. The founding fathers of the parties, who are supposed to be role models, are known to be working openly, or at times discretely, against the survival of their parties. Many politicians are not faithful to their party affiliation, depending on the political fortune of their group. The fickleness of party stalwarts, and the lack of ideological content and compatibility of the political parties and their members, discredits the integrity of the parties. The existing parties were formed out of the burning desire to get the military out of the political drama. In reality, the two "parties" in existence are probably the executives and legislative.[15] This is because there are no genuine parties with concrete ideologies. Thus, the integrity of political competition and participation continues to be in doubt in the Nigerian political process.

---

13. Dzurgba, 3–4.
14. Aina, *Party Politics in Nigeria*, 10.
15. Aina, 19–23.

Manipulation of Ethnic or Religious Sentiments

It is a fact that both ethnicity and religion are the most dangerous threats to the attainment of democratic politics in Nigeria. Ethnic groups are simply political action groups based on the principle of ethnicity. Ethnicity itself is a socially used cultural symbol. The very meaning of any ethnic identity can be found only at the borders; that is, in all the possible contacts in which a member of one ethnic group may come into contact with members of other such groups. Sometimes religious identity becomes part of an ethnic group's identity.[16]

In Nigerian political history, politicians, out of their selfish interest, have manipulated both ethnic and religious sentiments. For instance, the so-called religious riots in many parts of northern Nigeria are the external expression of these invisible hands of manipulation. Kukah opines that those who engage in this manipulation do so to cover up their lack of a political base. These politicians neither love their religion nor the people whom they claim to defend. In the end, according to Kukah, it is their personal and class interests that they seek to defend.[17] The limitations imposed by these self-serving and self-seeking politicians have marred national political integrity.

There are many Nigerians who feel so strongly about their religion that they are not ready to trade it for democratic talk. Within northern Nigeria, for instance, and especially within Islamic believers, there are many who see democratic politics as part of a worldly pursuit in which they cannot participate for fear of losing their religious kingdom.[18] Due to their low level of education and wrong concept of Western and secular ideas, democratic politics is often seen as part of the Western conspiracy to undermine Islam. Thus, on the surface, the mere thought of combining the elements of democratic politics with ethnicity and religion is enough to spark fire in the society. These are highly emotive issues over which blood has been spilled.[19] Tribes, cultures, and hope have been extinguished, and now more than ever before, new wars are being plotted and executed by politicians in this direction.

This manipulation is obvious in some northern states such as Kano, Zamfara, Sokoto and Katsina, where Islam was declared the state religion, in the name of democracy, undermining people of other faiths. Any opposition or the use of coercion by the federal government against such activities could have been seen as a violation of the right to freedom of religion, that is, the

---

16. Salamone, "Ethnic Identities and Religion," 45–46.
17. Kukah, *Democracy and Civil Society in Nigeria*, 25.
18. Kukah, 25.
19. Kukah, 26.

right of Muslims to practice sharia law in Nigeria.[20] Such opposition is enough to send the nation into chaos. This unscrupulous method used by politicians has caused religious and ethnic crises, which amount to the destruction of lives and properties in various parts of Nigeria. In destroying lives and properties, the people's right to life and property have been breached by fanatics who use ethnicity and religion to fight for the acquisition of political power and the control of human and material resources.[21]

The government could have been morally justified in using coercive measures to quell religious and ethnic riots. But the majority of the government has abused the moral and legal duties to protect life and property within the bounds of the law.[22] This is because many of them in power use the same methods to gain political power or office. Thus, there is a lack of integrity in Nigerian politics because moral virtues have been sacrificed on the altar of politics.

Imposition of Power by the Political Elites

Another cause of the decline of moral integrity is the establishment of hegemony and power in the Nigerian state. Hegemony is the leadership of one group over a group of others. In Nigerian politics, the process of establishing elite hegemony was initially not seen as a national project. Early in the independence era, the hegemonic interests that emerged were expressed within the boundaries of ethnic divisions to legitimize their rule.[23] This hegemonic style has affected both the military and civilian regimes since the beginning of the post-colonial state.

In the emergence of the nascent democracy in Nigerian politics, the political stalwarts tended to establish a new style of hegemonies around the upper classes of retired military men and their civilian counterparts.[24] This process of the establishment of a ruling class hegemony is designed in such a way as to make their stronghold survive well beyond the period of their stay in office. We have witnessed a situation where all those who had been in power, both military and civilian regimes, want to take over the reins of political power for a second or third time in the Third Republic. Having secured unlimited channels of exploitation, the ruling classes seek theoretical justification for the

---

20. Kukah, 26.
21. Dzurgba, *Nigerian Politics and Moral Behaviour*, 90.
22. Dzurgba, 90.
23. Kukah, *Democracy and Civil Society in Nigeria*, 41.
24. Kukah, 41.

status quo.[25] Profitable ventures that could have benefited the masses are either abandoned or sold to private sectors so that the suffering class could not catch up with the political hegemonies.

The political elites impose themselves as the only qualified and capable leaders in Nigerian democratic politics and want to rotate political powers among their hegemonies. They have established a political culture that will enable them to sustain their private establishments.[26] Thus, Nigerian politics is in the hands of a few who are there for their personal and groups' interests. For ordinary citizens, the nascent democracy in Nigeria is a ruthless struggle for power, a drama of bitter conflict of groups' interests, and of "who gets what, how, and when," and so on.[27] The old social vices in Nigerian political history of gross indiscipline on the part of those who are in public offices still remains the same. The political perennial vices, such as embezzlement of public funds, excessive greed, irresponsibility, lack of public accountability, tribalism, nepotism, and exploitation of the public good and welfare,[28] are still in full operation in the political life of the nation as well as in the socio-cultural life of the individuals. Hence, there is gross neglect of integrity in Nigerian politics, perpetrated mostly by political leaders and those in high places.

False Nationalism and Patriotism in Governance

Most Nigerian politicians have no spirit of patriotism and hence they cannot foster nationalism in their governance. Nationalism presupposes patriotism on the part of the citizens of the state, especially by those at the helm of affairs. *Nationalism* is when people believe that their country is the most important or the best, while *patriotism* refers to people's love for, and service to, their country.[29] A patriotic politician ought to love his or her country and be ready to defend it when the need arises. Such patriots see themselves as an integral part of the nation; the national goals, aspirations, progress, and problems are seen from their personal point of view, and this drives them to active involvement and participation in its affairs.[30]

---

25. Kukah, 42.
26. Kukah, 42.
27. Kukah, 42.
28. Kukah, 42.
29. *Longman Dictionary of Contemporary English.*
30. Kukah, *Democracy and Civil Society in Nigeria*, 57.

It is in the spirit of love and service that politicians ought to serve the nation and the common good of the people. But what we see in Nigerian politics is an unpatriotic attitude, people exhibiting disorderliness, instability, insecurity, and chaos, when their self-interests are thwarted. Nigerian "patriotic politicians" react in the opposite direction of patriotic nationalists when criticized by their fellow citizens.[31] Nigerian patriots prefer violence and intimidation to dialogue when it comes to issues that affect them. When a decision is not in their favor, they threaten national secession as the only viable solution to national issues.

Thus, in Nigeria, we have false nationalism and patriotism. The political scene has shown innocent lives being offered to the gods of false nationalism across the country. Under the banner of nationalism many have been killed in the name of protests or protection.[32] The patriots are ready to sacrifice lives so as to protect socio-economic interests. But the common good of the people is not sought after; rather things are more valuable than the citizens' lives. There is a collapse of integrity in national polity because of the unwillingness or inability of the political leaders to rise to the responsibility, and to the challenge of personal patriotic examples, which are the hallmarks of nationalism.

Thus, one will agree with Achebe, that indeed,

> the Nigerian national has not really emerged. What is known as Nigeria is a political society held together by legal and geographical ties! The binding force of shared historical experience with its related growth is yet to be developed. A united political philosophy that shapes the thinking of all Nigerian citizens is not formulated. Hence, there is no common identity.[33]

Rather what we have is "tribalhood" – that is, loyalty to ones' tribe. With this lack of national identity it is difficult to propel moral integrity in the interests of all Nigerians. Those who ought to build patriotic nationalism into Nigerian politics and governance have personalized politics to the detriment of the well-being of the common people.

Inability of Politicians to Accept Losing an Election

Another contributing factor to moral bankruptcy in Nigerian politics is the inability of an average Nigerian politician to know how to accept failure as

---

31. Kukah, 57.
32. Kukah, 57.
33. Achebe, *Trouble with Nigeria*, 7.

far as the contest for office is concerned.³⁴ In politics the creation of parties presupposes elections. An electoral commission creates constituencies and organizes elections through which the people select their representatives to local government councils, state assemblies, and the national assembly.³⁵

Elections perform some vital functions. They enable the citizens to select people of their choice. Elections disseminate information, which enables the entire society to know what is going on in national politics. In an ideal situation, elections ought to promote sociable tendencies among individuals and groups.³⁶ Thus, during elections, individuals and groups are compelled by common opinions and interests to minimize their prejudices and hatred in order to show friendliness to as many people as possible. In this way elections help to integrate individual Nigerians and groups into a common consciousness of one national identity. This is essential especially in a case where the whole nation has one constituency for some offices such as those of the president and the vice-president.³⁷

But most Nigerian politicians see elections as do-or-die affairs. Those who lose elections blame their opponents, local government, state government, the Electoral Commission, the polling booth, the day and time of the election, the weather, etc. Some of them, with a spirit of suspicion, may resort to traditional methods (like consulting with a witchdoctor) when the going gets really tough and conventional means fail.³⁸ The interpretation of fortune or misfortune in any venture could be hinged on seemingly innocuous things, such as the time of day, gender, or physical state of the first person sighted in the day – a blind or lame person, a snake crossing his or her path from the left or right, etc. "As such, the political space is sometimes a pantheon inhabited by 'deities' of various shapes, sizes, persuasions, or tongues."³⁹

Election or voting is a time of contention between politicians, parties, and pressure groups. Contention is a disagreement, fight or conflict arising when two or more politicians or political parties seek to possess one and the same office. In doing so, they may hold incompatible goals or choose to use incompatible means for achieving their goals. Each of the politicians feels that his or her goals or means of achievement is being threatened or hindered by the

---

34. Kukah, *Democracy and Civil Society in Nigeria*, 3.
35. Dzurgba, *Nigerian Politics and Moral Behaviour*, 2.
36. Dzurgba, 2.
37. Dzurgba, 2.
38. Kukah, *Democracy and Civil Society in Nigeria*, 3.
39. Kukah, 3.

activities or actions of his or her political rivals. Such initial perceptions may not arise from actual events, but rather from personal anxieties, prejudices, insecurity, or hatred.[40] However, the politicians involved become rivals who pursue their goals by using means ranging from persuasion to physical combat. Along this line, Dzurgba opines that contention is, therefore, characterized by arguments, abuses, and manipulation of the surrounding circumstances. Contestants believe that their lives and prosperity should be protected from destruction by their political rivals. When defensive, obstructive, and destructive attempts are made simultaneously, a contention becomes a crisis, which is always the scene of Nigerian politics at the time of elections. This eventually brings about a breakdown of law and order.[41] Thus, a series of election crises has led to loss of integrity in Nigerian politics.

Election crises result from the inability of Nigerian politicians to understand that being a gallant loser or a magnanimous victor lays the foundation on which political democracy is built. To Nigerian politicians, losing an election is the handiwork of evil, extra-terrestrial species or their agents, employed on earth by the enemy. That is why the common expression of a gallant loser in any election is "I was rigged out, the enemies have done their worst, etc." The electoral conduct of Nigerian politics and its violent characteristics lie in the unrealistic expectations of the participants and the observers.[42] The anarchical behavior of politicians during elections has marred the integrity of Nigerian politics.

Lust for Materialism

Nigeria is in an era of politics of "wealth for self," which is the pursuit of one's own pleasure as the highest and all-encompassing good.[43] Nigerian politicians operate a self-centered nationalism, the policies of corporate egoism. Politics becomes a means to an individual's selfish ends. Today what is called national interest in democratic politics is sometimes billed as the path, if not to personal affluence, at least to fulfillment, happiness, and much else that the politician might desire for self. Thus egoism runs rampant in Nigerian politics.

What makes political egoism so attractive? Undoubtedly, it is the fact that in all of us, politicians and non-politicians alike, there runs a strain of

---

40. Kukah, 3.
41. Dzurgba, *Nigerian Politics and Moral Behaviour*, 3.
42. Kukah, *Democracy and Civil Society in Nigeria*, 3.
43. Holmes, *Ethics*, 32.

self-centeredness; we are motivated at least in part by our own self-interest. The politics of self-centeredness leads to materialism. Materialism is the belief that "human actions are governed by the wish to gain things for oneself."[44] It is the popular idea that it is money, not God, that makes the world go around, hence the popular adage "money answers all things." It is in this direction, Karl Marx argued, that the material conditions of life determine economic and political life, and he saw them as shaping history even by convulsive change as reality broke through on the ideological constructs, which political classes had imposed on society.[45]

Thus political egoism and materialism imply that money is the basic engine of human action, especially in political action – that the end of life is to buy goods for personal consumption or pleasure. In this view, "money is politics and politics is money."[46] This is the kind of mentality we see among Nigerian politicians. Hence we have wealthy Nigerians who dominate or hijack political parties. Those with money and power rule most of the time irrespective of their level of moral integrity. In elections we see and read increasing reports from national dailies that "money-bag" politicians influence the elections and indirectly rig them in the name of political stability. Moral values are replaced by material or money values. The prudent who may likely have no financial influence are pushed aside, while more corrupt politicians are joining hands in the crusade to "cheat the government and enrich themselves quick. They are desirous to loot the treasury and recoup their election losses or expenses."[47] In this way political egoism and materialism contribute to the neglect of integrity in Nigerian politics.

Nonchalant Attitude of Christians to Politics

Another contributing factor or cause for moral neglect in Nigerian politics is the apolitical attitude of the majority of Nigerian Christians. The notion is that the Christian faith has nothing to do with politics. Christianity came to a number of the poly-ethnic societies now called "Nigeria" as far back as the seventeenth century, especially by the Portuguese missionaries. Even before the concept of Nigeria as a nation was born, Christianity had spread through the length and breadth of the country. Yet Christianity has not been felt

---

44. *Longman Dictionary of Contemporary English*, s.v. "materialism."
45. Storkey, "Materialism," 575–576.
46. Storkey, 575–576.
47. Storkey, 576.

much in national politics because of the nonchalant attitude of Christians to political activities. Christian missions, both foreign and indigenous, have been concerned with individual conversions and have left individuals to struggle in the midst of social vices in the politics of Nigeria. They separated politics from the social ministry of the church.

Christian missions went as far as establishing schools and hospitals, sending relief to Christian communities, and rendering all kinds of social services to individuals and families. They have been involved in all kinds of philanthropic activities and works of mercy. But they failed to remove the causes of human need, ignored the political and economic activities by non-involvement in transforming the structures of society, and did not take action for justice, which they preach. They failed to act as the agent of light and salt in the political arena of the nation. They failed to champion integrity in politics, hence, the moral vices in politics.

Effects of Moral Bankruptcy in Nigerian Politics

"Righteousness exalts a nation, but sin is a disgrace to *any* people" (Prov 14:34). The perversion of integrity in Nigerian politics has caused a lot of instability in the country. The adverse effects of the negligence of moral virtues are telling on national stability and development. The key word for moral failure in the Nigerian state is instability. Instability in our national context is the product of impoverished social change and rapid mobilization of new groups into Nigerian politics coupled with slow developments of political institutions. It is inconsistency or disequilibria in the consultative and regulative socio-ethical rules. Instability also changes within systems, which do not confirm to or proceed from moral rules governing organizational processes in the country.[48] Some of the results of moral perversion as they have affected the consistency of government programs in Nigeria will be discussed.

Political Instability and National Disintegration

The neglect of integrity has affected political stability and national integration. Because of the political corruption exhibited by those elected into power, there seems to be a lack of an enduring democratic political culture. Nigerians embraced democratic politics as if it was an end in itself. It takes men and

---

48. Nwosu, "Political Leadership and Instability," 70.

women of integrity for democracy to function.[49] Democracy is said to be like motherhood, because it enjoys support from everyone, and even those who only pay lip service to it do not deny its appeal. But there are some basic elements of democracy that make it functional: citizen involvement in political decision-making; some measure of equality among citizens; some degree of liberty or freedom granted to or retained by citizens; a system of representation; rule of law; an electoral system with majority rule; and education, especially in moral politics.[50] But in practice, the rules that govern the game are pushed aside.

Rigging in elections, for instance, is a violation of such democratic rules. It is electoral fraud, which includes altering or disregarding electoral rules, and modifying or violating electoral procedures. In Nigerian elections, illegal ballot papers are acquired, nominations of opponents are prevented, opponents are sometimes eliminated, voters are bribed with money and jobs, there is open voting instead of secret voting, and opponents' votes are destroyed. Thus electoral fraud leads to the recruitment of vandals, arsonists, assassins, and criminals.[51] Election results are predetermined – victory by landslide, moonslide, or mudslide – nothing is to get in the way of that victory for the party in power.[52] These moral vices contribute to instability and national disintegration. When political leaders lack integrity, political stability and national integration are at stake.[53] Citizens will lose interest in politics and government matters.

When political integrity is faulty, national integration will be difficult, and that implies a lack of political culture. The defect of integrity has denied the nation a common political culture. The inability for the political elite to find areas for building consensus over certain aspects of life such as truth, honesty, and respect amount to disunity or disintegration.[54] Integrity in politics unites the members of society as a whole. This will enable them to have a cultural identity. Culture has a way of confronting one another, sometimes counter-penetrating, inter-connecting, or intersecting. Though some forms of cultural expressions or language may be offensive to others, by and large, a society can always find an overarching value around which these differences can be negotiated.[55] This is what has happened with nearly all the civilizations of the

---

49. Nwosu, 70.
50. Oyediran, *Introduction to Political Science*, 36–37.
51. Dzurgbe, *Nigerian Politics and Moral Behaviour*, 60.
52. Soyinka, "Engaging the Past," 44.
53. Soyinka, 44.
54. Kukah, *Democracy and Civil Society in Nigeria*, 28.
55. Kukah, 28.

world. So what Nigerians need are political leaders with enough imagination and selflessness to enable the nation to find a rallying point around which nationalists can alter their differences so as to achieve national integration and greatness. But moral vices in politics have denied the nation such a vision.

Emergence of Political Godfathers

The absence of moral and political integrity in Nigerian democracy has resulted in the manipulation of power by those who assume the title of "the owners of Nigeria."[56] In Nigeria, we have a heritage of godfathers, those who believe that it is their God-given right to rule or to decide who will rule. We have these godfathers at all levels of governance – local, state and federal.[57] These are political elites who decide the fate of the nation. The inheritors are small groups of Nigerians who are closely united and do not allow others easily to join their group.

These governing inheritors have established themselves locally and internationally and no one dares to challenge them. Some people have testified that the inheritors or godfathers are the ones who deliberately fuel the national crises to ensure that the people do not speak with one voice to demand fairer treatment and their rights as citizens. They hinder Nigerians from electing capable leadership. They manipulate their own candidates into leadership in order to maintain the status quo. Thus, Nigeria lacks good leaders.[58] Nigeria actually has all the resources it needs, especially in terms of human and natural resources, to be a healthy, vibrant nation, if not for the godfather syndrome.

We have abundant human resources who can work for the benefit of the people of this country.[59] Nigerians excel abroad and are winning prizes. For example, Nigerian doctors and nurses and are well-respected overseas while the country's medical system collapses at home.[60] But because we lack political integrity in Nigerian leadership, democracy is failing again in Nigeria.

---

56. Adebanjo, "The Inheritors," 3.
57. Adebanjo, 3.
58. Adebanjo, 3.
59. Adebanjo, 3.
60. Sagay, "A Nation, Its Problems and Capable Leadership," 9.

Suppression of Human Rights and Values

The exclusion of moral rules in politics has brought about dehumanization in Nigeria. Dehumanization here refers to "the loss or suppression of characteristically human traits such as dignity, freedom, spontaneity, creativity, love and the capacity to worship."[61] Contemporary democratic politics in Nigeria is said to be dehumanizing, since it often lacks opportunities for significant achievements, creative work, and meaningful involvement. Particularly in the post-military civilian governance, Nigerians have called attention to the effects of a conformist, regimented society and its consumerism, which suppresses individual integrity in the process of providing a remarkable high standard of material comfort.

Nigerians were experiencing a "democratic dictatorship" because of the presence of the civilianized military politicians. A dictator has no respect of human life or rule of laws. Nigerians expected the Obasanjo's administration to attempt "to restore morals, to properly restructure the political system, to re-plant and nurture the institutions of democracy and to create a favorable atmosphere for democracy to flourish in."[62] What is further expected of the government is

> to strengthen judicial institutions and restore respect for the rule of law, to streamline the constitution and make it a satisfactory fundamental law of the land, sensitive to the needs of the multi-ethnic, multi-linguistic, multi-religious, pluralistic nation, to demarcate the responsibilities of the various tiers of government, and to neatly separate the powers and responsibilities of the executive, the legislative and the judiciary.[63]

But what we are experiencing in Nigerian democracy is in the opposite direction.

The dehumanizing nature of politics is such that government of the day does not "encourage the culture of dialogue, debate, and consensus building, neither provides security of life and property in a land that has known great insecurities," not even-handed in its dealings with the citizens. The government has no evidence of honesty, transparency, and accountability in its actions and policies where previous military politicians had enthroned corruption, lack of accountability and wholesale looting of the treasury and national resources. There is no concrete "resolution of internal conflicts and problems," which

---

61. Fletcher, "Dehumanization," 291.
62. Obeiechina, "Democracy Is Failing Again in Nigeria," 13.
63. Obeiechina, 13.

ought to be a great priority over all other commitments after such a perennial "period of national turmoil and instability."[64]

A government with a sense of integrity cannot remain "impatient of dissent and insensitive to the deep cravings of the people for peace and security. . . . The spirit of democratic tolerance and disciplined discourse indispensable" in a democratic politics cannot germinate under such a dehumanized government.[65] "A general sense of insecurity, frustration and exasperation almost as bad as the harsher periods of military dictatorship has crept back into Nigerian" political life.[66] Using the Anambra State to buttress the dehumanized nature of the Nigerian situation, Obiechina writes:

> Nigerians were again becoming emotionally and physically battered, as they were during the dark periods of the country's history. There has been little accountability. A simple straightforward democratic ritual, like the holding of elections, was completely botched. The economy has remained in the doldrums, and political assassinations have become rampant . . . The democratic experiment is tottering towards collapse. Nowhere does this near-collapse of the experiment register more emphatically than in Anambra State where the Obasanjo presidency has been waging a war of attrition against the government of Chris Ngige. Governor Ngige has, for some strange reason, become the bête noir of the presidency, and, in consequence, the people of Anambra State have become virtual hostages to a federal government that ought to guarantee their securities, right, and freedoms. By a bizarre twist of cruel money, they are suffering an emasculation and dehumanization worse than they had known during the varied periods of military dictatorship.[67]

Judging from the Anambra episode, thugs and the reign of mob violence and terror is the characteristic of the democratic politics. All because there is a gross moral bankruptcy in high and low places of political authorities in the nation.

---

64. Obeiechina, 13.
65. Obeiechina, 13.
66. Obeiechina, 13.
67. Obeiechina, 13.

Government Delaying Tactics in Responding to the Dangerous State of Affairs

Another adverse effect of the lack of integrity in the Nigerian government is "brinkmanship politics" – the act of pushing a dangerous state of affairs to the limit of safety before the government's intervention.[68] Most of the major crises in Nigeria receive government attention at the brink of danger, perhaps when many lives and properties have already been destroyed, but not before.[69] The Obasanjo democratic government, rather than creating the much-expected stability, has unleashed very strong destabilizing forces with the potential of causing the break-up of the country. The government feels adamant or unconcerned about the prevalent inter-ethnic and sectional violence as well as the unprecedented economic decline, which have distressed the nation since 1999. All parts of Nigeria, in one way or the other, have experienced some form of inter-ethnic or religious violence.[70]

The inability of the government to intervene in crises at an appropriate time supports the activities of political criminals in Nigeria. It is ironic that the same government, which acted so "promptly" to suspend an elected governor and declare a state of emergency in Plateau State, failed to order the arrest of political thugs that went to the extent of abducting an elected state governor and burning government properties, including part of the governor's residence in the South East Zone of the country. In that same state, we had earlier witnessed the Agulari versus Umuleri war. In the Niger-Delta, we had Okerika versus Eleme, Ijaw versus Itsekiri, Ijaw versus Bini, Ogoni versus Indoni, and Itsekiri versus Urhobo. The militant activities of the Ijaw youth movement in the Niger Delta had added a dangerous dimension to acts of national instability. In the southwest, we had the Ife versus Modakeke, Ijero versus Ilaje, and the rampage of the Oodua People's Congress (OPC). The northern zones have been unstable in the country as well. We had the political sharia riots, the Bachama versus Hausa/Fulani crisis, and the Tarok versus Hausa/Fulani in the Yelwa Shendan area of Plateau State. The north has also become the epicenter of religious crises with political undertones, including the recent insurgence of Boko Haram in the northeast and Fulani herdsmen terrorizing the nation. The failure of the government to act quickly brought the nation to the brink of ruin in the affected areas.[71]

---

68. *Longman Dictionary of Contemporary English*, s.v. "brinkmanship."
69. Obeiechina, "Democracy Is Failing Again in Nigeria," 13.
70. Umar, "Politics," 23.
71. Umar, 23.

The brinkmanship or delaying tactics of Nigerian politics are overwhelming, with the suspicion that the political elites are the major culprits in our national moral problems. Hence, the government is unable to restore peace and order and to bring the culprits to justice (for example, the murder of chief Bola Ige, the then attorney general of justice). Federation Chief Dikibo, Henry Marshal, and some other lesser known politicians have taken political violence to a new height, yet nothing has been done by the government,[72] though many of the problems and crises predate the Obasanjo democratic government. But according to Umar, "one would think that it is on account of that rot that General Obasanjo was selected as the most qualified person who could pull the nation back from the precipice and to lead it to the Promised Land."[73] Indeed Obasanjo assured Nigerians in his own words that he came to "restore the years which the locusts had eaten." Yet, after more than five years of Obasanjo administration, things only worsened. It is therefore evident that his much-vaunted leadership skills lack moral integrity; they are only in the realm of political myth. That is why we are experiencing the politics of brinkmanship all over the country; it is a gross effect of the lack of integrity on the part of political elites, in particular.

Emergence of Rich Politicians in the Midst of Poverty

The politics of affluence in the midst of abject poverty is the outcome of moral decline in Nigerian politics.[74] In the larger Nigerian civil society, the race for fast wealth has driven many people to abandon the time-tested values of morality and integrity. For many Nigerians, all that is important is "money, money, and money." It does not matter anymore how money is made.[75] Money is the driving force that pushes most people into politics. We have a crop of politicians who are more interested in money than the people they represent. The National Assembly is an example of such politicians, who are more interested in their allowances than the welfare and happiness of the people that voted them in.[76]

We are in a democratic era when the politicians are living in affluence, having plenty of money and wealth, while many Nigerians are living below the poverty line. The national democratic dividends are so grossly perverted that

---

72. Umar, 23.
73. Umar, 23.
74. Umar, 23.
75. Oabarinsa, *TELL*, January 3, 2005, 50.
76. Umar, "Democracy Is Failing Again in Nigeria," 26.

less than 3 percent of the population controls over 60 percent of the national wealth, without adding any significant value to its productive base.[77] The operation of a single political economy, that is "oil polity," has depressed other more beneficial and elastic sectors, as the economy becomes more dependent on oil as its major engine of growth and source of government revenue. This, and the environmental degradation caused by oil extraction, have caused a strain between the oil-producing areas and the rest of the country. While those in government are living in affluence, the masses of the people in oil-producing areas are subject to chronic poverty.[78]

The Nigerian political elites have ensured poverty through their perfected divide-and-rule tactics, first initiated by the colonial masters. In its search for socio-political and economic advantage, the average member of the Nigerian elite will seek to reinforce the fears of members of his ethnic group, which he calls "my people." In their political tactics such politicians find ready scapegoats in the maladministration of governments. The leadership failure to exercise power justly and equitably serves ethnic jingoists very well. They readily seize on the situation to claim they are fighting in the interest of their people. Of course the real motive in most cases is personal aggrandizement and enrichment. These same elite will divert the revenue allocated to "my people" to their own personal account.[79]

While our politicians are displaying their wealth, their fellow citizens are struggling to obtain the basic necessities of life. The lack of integrity exhibited by those who have the keys to national wealth has caused their fellow human beings to suffer in the midst of plenty. These "poor masses are powerless to determine their own destinies and meet their own needs."[80] All because men and women with political power do not consider credibility, transparency, honor, and integrity as core values, which ought to count the most in their private and public life.[81]

Conclusion

In a nutshell, integrity is a missing ingredient in Nigerian politics. Lack of integrity has caused ceaseless conflicts and frustrations in the nascent

---

77. Umar, 27.
78. Umar.
79. Umar.
80. Bunting, "Poverty," 678.
81. Bunting, 678.

democracy in Nigeria, which has led some people to conclude that politics is a "dirty game" and is meant for deviants and criminals. In our assessment, the political crises in this great country have caused cultural, social, economic, intellectual, and spiritual suffering to its citizens. Many Nigerians, for instance, have suffered from lack of food, water, clothing, shelter, and health care, and have to deal with escalating inflation, abuse of political power, assassinations, oppression, and contempt. Citizens have lived in fear and uncertainty in the face of many unfulfilled promises and inflated hopes. Nigerian democratic politics have always been characterized by self-deceit, superficiality, materialism, greed, selfishness, and lust.[82]

Many citizens are disillusioned with the neglect of moral integrity in the politics of Nigeria. Is there any hope for this country? Can integrity be instilled in Nigerian politics? Can Nigerian politicians walk in godly integrity? The next chapter will answer these questions and propose possible solutions to the Nigerian political moral bankruptcy.

---

82. Dzurgba, *Nigerian Politics and Moral Behaviour*, 30.

6

Inculcation of Integrity into Nigerian Politics

Democratic politics as it is practiced in Nigeria is a form of government which rests on the assumption that human beings have the power of choice and that through the proper exercise of this capacity they may acquire those moral values without which life would not be worth living. In an ideal situation, democratic politics accepts as one of its basic principles the doctrine of the supreme worth of the individual; it cannot endorse or condone the suppression of personality for the sake of any other end. Like Kant's categorical imperative, it insists that every human being within its borders shall be treated as an end and never only as a means.[1]

This principle of the equal worth of all citizens is simply the right of each person to live in the knowledge that their value is equal to that of any other individual. In other words, no consideration of tribe, sub-tribe, religion, economic status, intellectual ability, or social standing shall interfere with the right of the individual to those elements which are essential to the development of his or her personality, except of course, those activities which may prevent a similar development on the part of others.[2] As has been said many times, integrity is an essential element in an ideal democratic politics. But how do we gain integrity in Nigerian politics? This is one of the questions this chapter intends to discuss.

It is for the sake of moral ideals, including integrity, and the possibility of their realization, that governments come into existence. The only valid test of good governance is to be found in the nature of the ideal and adequacy with which it can be used as a means for the fulfillment of that end. In this chapter

---
1. Helm, "Kant, Immanuel," 55.
2. Kukah, *Democracy and Civil Society in Nigeria*, 6.

we shall be concerned primarily with how to inculcate integrity into Nigerian politics. Accepting the ideal of the harmonious biblical concept of integrity as treated in chapter 1, we shall need to apply this value in some areas such as the politicians, political parties, government, electorates and the Christian faith. We begin our discussion with the politicians.

Politicians and Integrity

Having examined the causes and effects of moral negligence in Nigerian politics, one might ask, "How does a politician gain integrity?" It is not something we inherit from parents or receive at birth. Integrity is a homegrown moral virtue – it starts with our upbringing. For instance, the Christian home and church are the places where Christians are supposed to be educated and be holistically prepared for public life. Integrity encompasses both righteousness and justice. It is a right relationship with God and fellow human being. Integrity cannot be cultivated when a person is not living right with God, which is righteousness. When people are living right with their Maker, their righteousness will manifest itself in right relationships with their neighbors, which is justice. To have integrity in politics, therefore, means that every politician has to be right with God in their thoughts; they need to be right with God both in words and in deeds.[3] It is only then that integrity can be built in practical politics. Thus, a politician with sound integrity will realize that it is the right of every human being to enjoy the dignity, equality, and responsibility that comes with being created in the image of God in order to have right relationships with God, with fellow human beings, and with the material world.[4]

To further answer the "how" question, the psalmist says, "He who has clean hands and a pure heart, who does not trust in an idol or swear by a false god" (Ps 24:4). In this verse, the psalmist states four ways in which integrity can be inculcated into the life of a person.[5] This also applies to politicians.

1. Clean Hands in Politics

"Clean hands" here does not mean simply the dirt on a politician's hands. It means the *purity of deeds*. It also means what a politician does not do. Interestingly, the doctrine of clean hands is still used in secular law today:

---

3. Kukah.
4. Stott, *Issues Facing Christians Today*, 206.
5. Murphy and Murphy, *International Minister's Manual*, 67.

> When a plaintiff goes into a court of equity and asks the judge to do something on his behalf, the judge has the right to examine that plaintiff's own conduct in the matter. The plaintiff must be free of any guilty or contributing acts if he is to win over the defendant. This is referred to as the "Clean hands" doctrine.[6]

That is to say, the plaintiff must have clean hands to prevail.

Thus, we see this "clean hands" requirement both in the Bible and in secular law. In the biblical perspective, "clean hands" speaks volumes about the person; it encompasses their entire being. It means politicians do not indulge in the sins of the flesh. Politicians with integrity do no harm to their neighbors, rather they do what is right towards others, even their political opponents.[7] Morally sound politicians are not involved in murder, rape, or any act of sexual immorality; they do not lie, cheat, steal, slander, or embezzle public funds. It also implies that they do not yield their physical bodies to consistent lifestyle sins with such things as drug or alcohol abuse.

2. Pure Heart in Politics

The phrase "a pure heart" as the psalmist used it speaks of what a person thinks – one's inward thoughts. For example, when Jesus first saw Nathaniel, he said, "Now here is a genuine son of Israel – a man of complete integrity" (John 1:47 NLT). In other words, when Jesus saw Nathaniel, he knew that Nathaniel had a pure thought life.[8] Every politician should know that God knows our every thought. Impure thoughts, whether they come as a result of fallen human nature, or from a demon as some people believe, are not pleasing to God. As a person of integrity, as soon as such impure thoughts come, they must be rejected and put out of one's mind immediately.

By exercising this mental discipline hundreds or thousands of times, a politician develops the godly integrity of a pure heart that will be of help to him or her in practical politics. Why is God so concerned with our thought life? Because God knows that thought precedes action, whether good or bad, right or wrong. So to *act* with integrity a politician must *think* with integrity. Proverbs 27:19 says it succinctly: "As water reflects the face, so ones' life reflects the heart." Thus, politicians have to strive to show a sense of maturity, that is, an ability to impose self-discipline on their own thoughts, decisions,

---

6. Murphy and Murphy, 67.
7. Murphy and Murphy, 67.
8. Murphy and Murphy, 68.

emotions, behavior, and activity.⁹ Pure hearts demand patience, tolerance, and understanding in dealing with the public and with a variety of characters and problems.¹⁰

3. No Idolatry in Politics

Few politicians in today's Christian world have physical images or idols before which they bow down and worship. However, God's view of idolatry is reflected in Moses's writing of the decalogue:

> You shall have no other gods before me. You shall not make for yourself an image in the form of anything in heaven above or on the earth beneath or in the waters below. You shall not bow down to them or worship them, for I the LORD your God am a jealous God. (Exod 20:3–5a)

The positive side of this commandment says, "Love the LORD your God with all your heart and with all your soul and with all your strength" (Deut 6:5). Jesus himself reaffirms this commandment as the greatest commandment (Matt 22:36–38).¹¹

Therefore, foremost to every politician is God's command to love him with all their heart, soul, and mind. Anything that politicians love more than God, is their idol, like money, wealth, and position. Once any such things take the place of God, that person lacks godly integrity. Such politicians are able to do anything evil in order to worship his or her "gods." Integrity begins with total surrender to God's will for one's life and absolute trust in him. People must see political appointment as an opportunity for service to the glory of God. Such politicians who have the fear of God will not join cults or secret societies for security or protection. Neither will they be involved in ritual killings in order to acquire money, power, or position. An example of holistic integrity for politicians is to resolve to love the Almighty God with all their heart, soul, and mind, and to please him in any political appointment. Thus, such people will see their fellow politicians as one with the image of God and must be treated as such.

---

9. Dzurgba, *Nigerian Politics and Moral Behaviour*, 4.
10. Murphy and Murphy, *International Minister's Manual*, 68.
11. Murphy and Murphy, 69.

4. No Falsehood in Politics

A person of integrity should not "swear falsely." When we rationalize this phrase in the narrowest sense, what comes to mind is truth-telling under oath in a court of law. And certainly this requirement of truthfulness under oath is part of what this verse means ("swear by a false god," Ps 24:4c). However, this verse is more than just about telling the truth under oath.[12] It is a warning against such things as lying, treachery, perjury, forgery, and deception. It further warns against double-talk, empty talk, flattery, false promises, and false conduct.

The Lord God hates politicians who pretend, display lip-service only, show false sympathy and false piety, are involved in fraud and foul play, and the like. The book of Proverbs contains many admonitions about bearing false witness:

> There are six things the LORD hates,
> seven that are detestable to him:
> haughty eyes,
> a lying tongue,
> hands that shed innocent blood,
> a heart that devises wicked schemes,
> feet that are quick to rush into evil,
> a false witness who pours out lies
> and a person who stirs up conflict in the community.
> (Prov 6:16–19)

This is a vivid description of people who use their mouths, eyes, feet, and fingers in devious ways to achieve the deceitful plots of their hearts. In politics, it means especially that politicians ought not to spread falsehood about their opponents to destroy them.[13] Politicians ought to accept their shortcomings in humility, honesty, and sincerity, striving continually to win public trust and confidence through personal trustworthiness, reliability, and dependability.[14]

Acquisition of integrity demands living in peace with victorious opponents, and with policies one cannot change. Such politicians should strive to be calm in the face of unwarranted provocation, disappointment, and embarrassment. A moral politician upholds honor and preserves the rules of competition. Politicians of integrity will not get involved in things like the assassination of opponents or election rigging. They will refresh others so that they themselves will be refreshed in turn. Politicians who will not swear falsely or act falsely, will

---

12. Murphy and Murphy, 70.
13. Murphy and Murphy, 70.
14. Dzurgba, *Nigerian Politics and Moral Behaviour*, 4.

have the moral courage to face disapproval, even of their friends, for a course of action they were compelled to take on the grounds of principle and conscience. Such politicians of integrity understand the value and importance of patient persuasions in the process of lobbying, and understand as well that failure in a given election does not mark the end of their political career. Victories have often come about after many failures in the political scene.[15]

Politicians of integrity, instead of walking in the way of falsehood, will fight against corruption in all its forms – immorality, subversion, forgery, inefficiency, poor productivity, bribery, etc. – through their legislative power. Thus, it is expected that good politicians will serve their country with sound knowledge, goodwill, tolerance, cooperation, and compromise.[16]

In the Nigerian political arena, many politicians do not understand that integrity is the quality most needed to succeed in politics. Some politicians think they can do whatever they want, particularly with small issues, because they believe that as long as there are not any major problems, they are doing well. But ethical principles are not flexible. Integrity in the life of a politician is also about the small things, which often get pushed aside.[17]

A "little white lie" is still a lie. Theft is theft whether it's N100, N1000 or N10 million. Persons of integrity commit themselves to building character over personal gain, to people over things, to service over power, to principle over convenience, to the long view over the immediate. Character is built in the small moments of life. Anytime politicians break a moral principle, they create a small crack in the foundation of their integrity. And then, "when times get tough, it becomes harder to act with integrity, not easier. Character is not created in a crisis, it only comes to light."[18] Everything politicians have done in the past (or the things they have neglected to do), become glaring when they are under pressure.

Building Integrity in Political Life

Many Nigerians today are desperate for political leaders, but they want to be influenced only by individuals they can trust – politicians of good character. Politicians who want to become people who can positively influence others, need to develop the following qualities of integrity, stated by Maxwell and

---

15. Kukah, *Democracy and Civil Society in Nigeria*.
16. Dzurgba, *Nigerian Politics and Moral Behaviour*, 4.
17. Maxwell and Dornan, *Becoming a Person of Influence*, 1.
18. Maxwell and Dornan, 1.

Dornan, and live them out on a daily basis: model consistency of character, employ honest communication, value transparency, exemplify humility, demonstrate support of others, fulfil promises, embrace an attitude of service, and encourage two-way participation with people they influence politically.[19]

However, the development of integrity is an internal job. Integrity is not determined by circumstances nor based on credentials. Character comes from who a politician is. But most Nigerians would like to be judged not by who they are but by the titles they have earned or the positions they have held, irrespective of their character. Some politicians desire to influence their followers by the weight of their credentials rather than the strength of their moral character. No number of titles, degrees, offices, awards, or other credentials are a substitute for basic, honest integrity when it comes to the power of influencing others in an ideal democratic politics.[20]

Developing Spiritual Integrity

Contemporary politicians in Nigeria need to develop "spiritual integrity."[21] To be contemporary is to live in the present, and to move with the times, without necessarily being concerned with either the past or the future. To be a "contemporary politician," is to ensure that the present is enriching to the fullest possible extent both by one's knowledge of the past and the expectation of the future. Contemporary politics, globally, demands this. There are contemporary politicians all over the world who are trusting and worshiping God, the "the Alpha and the Omega . . . who is, and who was, and who is to come" (Rev 1:8). And the Lord Jesus Christ to whom these politicians are committed to is "the same yesterday and today and forever" (Heb 13:8).

Nigerian politicians should trust in God, their Maker, and not in their ancestors, charms, and juju or human ritual killings, in order to succeed in politics. God is behind politics and a wise politician must be submissive to God's biblical authority in politics.[22] Many Nigerians would immediately deny this statement and even affirm the contrary. They cannot understand how apparently intelligent Christians of the Western world at the end of the twentieth century can possibly be so perverse as to believe in biblical

---

19. Maxwell and Dornan, 22–23.
20. Maxwell and Dornan, 22–23.
21. Stott, *Contemporary Christian*, 177.
22. Stott, 177.

inspiration and authority.[23] Nigerian politicians may regard a commitment to the truth and trustworthiness of Christian Scripture as untenable in Nigerian politics. But they fail to recognize how Christian teachings based on the word of God have transformed and are still transforming global politics.[24]

Integrity, which is the quality of a well-integrated politician, can only be fully attained through faith in God. In particular, integrated Christian politicians are at peace, not at war, with themselves. There is an inner harmony as they go about their political activities. What is the secret of this integration? It is the biblical affirmation that "Jesus Christ is Lord." He is the Lord of human politics. It is the essence of integrated discipleship that Christians both confess his lordship with their lips and enthrone him as Lord in their hearts. Biblical Christianity assumes the yoke of Christ's teaching authority. Christians seek to take "every thought captive to the obedience of Christ" (2 Cor 10:5). And when Jesus is Lord of their beliefs, opinions, ambitions, standards, and values then they are integrated Christian politicians, since that is when "integrity" will mark their political life. Only when he is Lord do we become whole.[25]

> Jesus our Lord himself submitted to the Old Testament Scriptures. In his ethical conduct, in his understanding of his mission, and in his public debates with contemporary religious leaders, his primary concern was to be true to Scripture. "What does the Scripture say?" he would ask. It was always his final court of appeal. And he expected his disciples to follow his example in this. He also made provision . . . [for] the New Testament to be written, by choosing, calling, equipping and commissioning his apostles to be the teachers of the church [his "political party"], and he expected the church to submit to them.[26]

Thus, the way to gain spiritual integrity in Nigerian politics is to determine to retain our conviction about God's love, in spite of the residual difficulties, ultimately for one reason only, namely, that Jesus our Lord himself taught it and exhibited it. It was because of Jesus that all came to believe in God's love in the first place; it is for the same reason that we should continue to do so,

---

23. Stott, 177.
24. Stott, 179.
25. Stott, 177.
26. Stott, 177–178.

even in our political lives. "It is more than faith; it is the sober, intellectual and spiritual integrity of confessing Jesus as Lord,"[27] even in Nigerian politics.

Being Power Servant Politicians

A person of integrity will be a *power servant* rather than a *power broker*. There is no doubt about it – politics is power. When a person has the decision-making authority over many people and the willingness of those people to abide by the decision, that person has power. Indeed, the fact that politics is power is what attracts many Nigerians to political activism. "It is exciting to be where the action is, where history is being made, and where impact for the better is made on people's lives and livelihoods. Power is exciting, but it is also an addicting narcotic of the psyche."[28] Some Nigerian politicians become so hooked on it that they would sell their very souls to Satan in order to be elected or selected to serve on some prestigious office holder's staff in a decision-making position. This may be what brought about the phrase "political animal," which unfortunately, some Nigerian politicians and political activists have become. They sacrifice their integrity just to stay in positions of power. These politicians fight and struggle, they do things they would never have imagined themselves doing, in order to beat their opponents and live under the intoxicating influence of political power.[29] This should not be! Politics is not a "do or die" affair! It is not for personal aggrandizement or to advance one's own interest. Political power exists not to be used selfishly but to be entrusted to those who can be counted on to advance the good of the democratic society.

Many Nigerian politicians, including those who have now been corrupted by political power, entered the political arena in hopes of filling a need. But these people's egos are generally enormous – political power becomes the way to enhance their self-esteem. Consequently they use their political power selfishly.[30] Nigerian politicians must encounter the Christ of the Bible to fill the vacuum within their lives, which political positions cannot fill. Christians, for example, are people who are supposed to know the full acceptance and approval of God himself. The void within is filled with the presence of the Holy Spirit. Their direction in life is clear as they walk according to the commands of their master, Jesus. They are true citizens of Nigeria who need not prove

---

27. Stott, 180.
28. Elder, "Politics and Christian Discipleship," 133.
29. Elder, 133.
30. Elder, 134.

themselves to anyone. Even Christians who are politicians are not supposed to be power hungry, because they are at peace with God and with their fellow Nigerians, irrespective of tribe or religion or party. They are also at peace with themselves. Because of these personal characteristics and sound integrity endowed to them by God, they are excellent candidates for handling Nigerian political power responsibly.

Thus, a politician needs to be a follower of Jesus Christ and to be able to exhibit a servant role in political life, because that is exactly the way to develop integrity and the right attitude for handling the political power entrusted to a public *servant* for appropriate administration of that power.[31] In other words, as stated earlier, politicians ought to be *power servants* rather than *power brokers*, if they want to serve with integrity in the Nigerian political scene.

Political Parties and Integrity

Political parties are the outcome of the modernization of political systems. They are a recent development in human management of society. Whether in one-party, two-party, or multi-party systems, the political parties ought to behave in theory and practice as a "legal person" of sorts. As such, every political party should be morally guided and have a moral conscience. However, political parties are defined as "organizations that seek to attract the support of the general public in a political system."[32] Such parties play a direct and substantial role in political recruitment and are often interested in the capture of political power at local, state, or federal level, either alone or in coalition with others.

Political parties were introduced in Nigeria in May 1999. Eleven political parties were recognized but only three were prominent. These were the Peoples Democratic Party (PDP), the All Peoples Party (APP), and the Alliance for Democracy (AD). After much struggle with the INEC, many more political associations were recognized to contest the April 2003 series of elections. Only twenty of the thirty political parties nominated presidential candidates.[33] The mood and behavior of the political parties was childish. We are reminded of Paul's words in 1 Corinthians 13:11 where he talks about childish speech, understanding, and thought. Some of these parties were thoughtlessly and carelessly formulated with lots of excitement but a lack of in-depth understanding. The thinking was vague and unrealistic.

---

31. Elder, 134.
32. Oyediran, *Introduction to Political Science*, 52.
33. Oyediran, 60.

Political integrity demands that any political party should exhibit certain major characteristics such as the continuity of an organization. The intention should be that the party will span the life of its current leaders and members, and seek permanence at all levels of government with regular communication between these levels. The party must consciously seek to win election at all levels and constantly seek new members and supporters. Thus, to inculcate moral integrity in Nigerian political parties, their functions must: include aggregate interests and opinions; link the government with the governed; widen political participation; educate, enlighten, integrate and mobilize the populace; set goals and values for the society; and nominate and recruit into public office.[34]

To prove the integrity of a political party, its constitution and membership should cut across ethnic and religious differences. Its leadership should be nominated and elected from time to time through its constitutional methods. No members or group of members should be allowed to dominate the party or run it as a private company. It is a moral mandate for any political party to build in its members a sense of honor, dignity, honesty, integrity, and accountability. This means as well that a political party should not tolerate corruption for fear of losing support or an election.[35]

Political Parties Must Treat Each Other with Integrity

The integrity of a political party demands mutual partnership with other political parties. A party ought not to undermine the peace, order, and stability of other political parties but should practice healthy competition, mutual understanding, tolerance, cooperation, and constitutional ideals – all working together to promote a democratic political scene of integrity. Each party should see itself as unique and having a meaningful contribution in Nigerian polity.[36] There is a need for each party to understand and appreciate that its responsibility to the electorate does not lie solely in its assuming national leadership. Outside of government, it may even do better in shaping the course of public affairs. Instead of seeing each other as enemies, the party in power should exercise their responsibility to the people.[37]

---

34. Oyediran, 52–53.
35. Dzurgba, *Nigerian Politics and Moral Behaviour*, 69.
36. Dzurgba, 69.
37. Dzurgba, 70.

To become a political party of integrity, the party needs to go back to the fundamentals. It has to strive to respect the principle of democracy. The democratic principle is the political expression of persuasion by argument. In a democratic society, political parties, whether in power or not, need to maintain and foster the time aspects of the decision-making process. The first concerns *who* takes the decision. "A decision is democratically taken if the answer to the question of 'who takes it?' is 'more or less everybody,' in contrast to decisions taken only by those best qualified to take them"[38] or who feel it is their right. "Second, democracy describes *how* a decision is reached. 'A decision is taken democratically if it is reached by discussion, criticism and compromise.' Third, democracy describes *the spirit* in which a decision is made, namely 'being concerned with the interests of all, instead of only a faction or a party.'"[39] A political party exists to promote this democratic principle, which also reflects the balanced biblical view of human beings.[40] All political parties should have this in mind in all their activities.

Political Parties Must Treat the Public with Integrity

The political party should not only be concerned with the question of winning the public debate or vote, but of securing legislation that will make public life more pleasing to God. That is to say that moral integrity demands the political party's involvement in social action. The main function of the political party is to formulate polity or law that will safeguard the accepted values of society and protect the rights of citizens. By so doing such a political party will enjoy public approval and support during election. It is a lack of integrity that causes some party members to buy votes by giving money or gifts to the public. A party with sound moral integrity will work to implement some of its manifestos for the welfare of the masses, even when not in power, rather than waiting to do that work when elected. Money often used for bribing or the hiring of political thugs, could be used for the benefit of the citizens, which will eventually attract public support. In other words, integrity propels political parties to be involved in political action, which is love seeking justice for the oppressed.

---

38. Stott, *Issues Facing Christians Today*, 40.
39. Stott, 40.
40. Stott, 41.

Members of Political Parties Must Act with Integrity

Members of any political party have unique resources to bring into political dialogue. Participation in a political party and concerned citizens' groups help accomplish what one person could never do alone. Thus, each member's participation in the political process should grow into year-round activity.[41] People should continually be open to new ideas and more personal political involvement. In other words, each member should act with integrity. Integrity in all phases of influencing, reporting, campaigning, and voting are imperative to the political party. The moral norms of love and justice should be kept in mind. Issues must be dealt with in terms of the people behind them. Political parties should work for the good of all persons and to the glory of God, as such parties come to consider themselves not only as loyal, patriotic *national* parties but also as *global* parties as well.[42]

Role of the Nigerian Government

In contemporary Nigeria, "government" is wrongly used to refer to the executive branch of the state in distinction to its legislative and judicial branches. In this section, the term "government" will refer more broadly to "political authorities," whatever their precise institutional form.[43] Thus, there is a need to answer the question, what is government? Government is the organization that protects, provides services, and supervises the affairs of a group of people who are organized into a legal, identifiable, political body. At the federal level, the government consists of the president, his cabinet, and the appointed officials who work closely with him. At the state and local levels, government includes all elected officials such as governors, legislators, local government chairmen, counselors, and the appointees who work for them. Generally, the government includes all those who are employed by the government, including all people in the civil, judicial, and military and other public services.[44]

Government exists for the promotion of the well-being of all in society. In the previous chapters, we discussed the serious neglect of integrity as a result of long-term bad governance in Nigeria. To worsen the situation, most Nigerians often regard government as an external body in which they do not play any part. When such people visualize the government they exclude themselves

---

41. Tillman, *Christian Ethics*, 108.
42. Tillman, 109.
43. Chaplin, "Government," 415–417.
44. Ozodo, *Nigeria Covenant*, 65.

from the picture. Therefore, though they feel free to criticize the shortcomings of the government, such Nigerians often do not see that they have any direct role to play in improving the situation.[45] They do not realize that they are part of the problem. Therefore, we will now consider *how* to inculcate integrity into the governance in Nigeria. This will be achieved under three main sub-topics: (1) government bearing the banner of integrity; (2) government integrity as God's servants; and (3) government integrity as public servants, which applies to all three levels of government – local, state and federal.

Government Ought to Bear the Banner of Integrity

The Nigerian government ought to bear the banner of integrity and protect its citizens from injustice and moral decadence. The key question is: What does the government do? Or what is the purpose of government? Though there are a lot of opinions about this issue, there is general agreement that the Nigerian government exists for the promotion of the well-being of *all* Nigerians. By nature, each individual seeks his or her own personal well-being. In order to optimize that well-being, most Nigerians are willing to submit themselves to regulations made on behalf of the entire nation-state. Those specifically selected or elected to make or supervise the observance of such regulations constitute the government. Their moral responsibilities include the maintenance of law and order as stated by the Apostle Peter:

> Submit yourselves for the Lord's sake to every human institution, whether to a king as the one in authority, or to governors as sent by him for the punishment of evildoers and the praise of those who do right. (1 Pet 2:13–14)

The government should also be involved in the welfare schemes of their people (see Gen 41:46–49, 53–57). The bottom line is that integrity demands the promotion of the well-being or good life of the people they govern.[46] But if one accepts a government role in promoting the citizens' welfare, what are the legitimate means of accomplishing this in a democratic society? The means for bringing about moral integrity or social change through government action with democratic politics are available through all three arms of government –

---

45. Ozodo, 65.
46. Ozodo, 65.

executive, legislative, and judicial. Moral integrity needs to be instilled in these various arms of government.[47]

Moral integrity has to commence from the *legislative* arm of government. This is because election is a very critical element of the legislature. The primary responsibility of the legislature is to make laws for the smooth and effective running of a nation. In Nigerian governments, the central legislature is called the National Assembly (since the 1999 Constitution) and this central legislature is made up of the House of Representatives and the Senate. The integrity of the legislatures is crucial to the national life of society.[48] The legislature receives bills from either its members or the executive arm of government. Integrity demands that these bills should be thoroughly examined and passed through various stages without any selfish interest. The bills can be altered, through addition or deletion. It is the view of the majority of the members of the legislature that either becomes law or is sent to the executive for assent before it becomes the law. Integrity enhances an effective administration of the bills and the manner in which they are implemented. Thus moral integrity is paramount on the part of the legislature. This is because the very essence of representative government is the legislature.[49]

The legislative arms of the government are tribal or ethnic ambassadors of the varied citizens of the various tribes making up a nation-state. They are the mirrors of Nigeria as a nation. Crucial decisions are made by the legislature. When legislators make laws, they do so as ambassadors, as the people's representatives.[50] When the legislature lacks the integrity expected of them, their people clamor to take some decisions on their own, not through their representatives. Thus integrity must be maintained to influence those in office to enact objective laws because electing the "right" legislators may not assure that they will vote "right."[51] It takes men and women of integrity to enact genuine laws and at the same time become agents of moral change.

Integrity of the *executive* arm of government is also highly needed. A real executive directs the business of government. The executive arm of government often recommends and initiates bills, which are considered by the legislature. But veto power often belongs to the executive, most especially in a presidential system of government, which Nigeria practices. In Nigeria's political system,

---

47. McQuilkin, *Introduction to Biblical Ethics*, 80.
48. Oyediran, *Introduction to Political Science*, 28.
49. Oyediran, 29.
50. Oyediran, 30.
51. McQuilkin, *Introduction to Biblical Ethics*, 481.

the powers to call the legislature and the power to dissolve it belong to the executive. It directs and supervises the execution of laws; it is responsible for appointing and removing members of the cabinet, the ministers.[52] Thus, for a person to assume such authority, they should be of sound integrity who will not abuse their power against those who elected them.

The executive has the mandate to promote integrity at various arms and levels of government because of its legislative, administrative, and judicial functions. It holds the key components of government such as order, justice, and freedom. Integrity demands that the executive administers peace, and orders justice and freedom in society.[53]

The *judiciary* is another arm of government. Its basic responsibility is to adjudicate in disputes between the other arms of government – the legislative and the executive – or between the citizens and government, or between citizens. Integrity and fairness in the performance of its duties are very critical. A judiciary with honest, knowledgeable, and impartial judges of integrity ought to be a great asset to Nigeria and its people. The integrity on the part of the judiciary is to interpret the constitution fairly, and to settle disputes without bribes and with fair judgement.[54] It is their moral duty to punish those who break the law and to protect citizens against arbitrary laws and abuse of power.

It is the moral duty of the judiciary arm of government to provide justice for the citizens. Indeed, order and justice are necessary for the restraint of moral neglect, injustice, and disorder. Human sinfulness must be curtailed within certain limits for the preservation of civic and communal life. The courts of justice and the police forces are instituted as instruments for enforcing the law of the land.[55] That is why the judicial arm of the government cannot be lacking in integrity. To insure moral integrity in government, it is essential that the judiciary be independent, because this is essential to individual freedom. Oyediran writes that,

> the appointment of judges must be made by impartial bodies such as judicial service commission, tenure must be secure; remuneration must be from consolidate funds not from any executive appropriation and must make judges reasonably comfortable.[56]

---

52. Oyediran, *Introduction to Political Science*, 32.
53. Kunhiyop, *African Christian Ethics*, 110.
54. Oyediran, *Introduction to Political Science*, 4.
55. Kunhiyop, *African Christian Ethics*, 112.
56. Oyediran, *Introduction to Political Science*, 35.

If this step is taken, the integrity of the judiciary as an instrument of justice will be a boost for civil society and democratic politics in Nigeria.

Democratic integrity of government demands checks and balances among the various arms of government. That is, an arrangement whereby any arm or branch of government – legislative, executive or judiciary – serves as a check on another arm of government. This is to prevent abuse of power, which will at the end tarnish the integrity of the government. What this means is that when the legislative branch makes laws, it is another branch of government that executes the law and another that interprets it.[57] This will help to improve the integrity of the three arms of government.

Government as God's Servant

The integrity of those in government will improve when they realize that God ordains government. From a biblical perspective, government is consistently seen as instituted, authorized, and circumscribed by God, and its legitimacy is dependent upon the proper exercise of that authority, the purpose of which may be formulated as the establishment of justice in the public realm of society.[58] Every human government has divine origin. It is against this background that Paul's acknowledgement of the divine origin of Roman political authority (Rom 13:1–7), and Peter's (1 Pet 2:13–14), must be viewed. God has authorized the office of government as "a minister of God to you for good" (Rom 13:4a), and specifically, "for the punishment of evildoers and the praise of those who do right" (1 Pet 2:14).[59]

The Nigerian government functions on behalf of God. No political leaders can boast that it is through their hard work that a democratic government is formed or established. Nigerian politics exists for the glory of God and for the good of all Nigerians. Thus those in political authority are servants of God and they are accountable to him in whatever way they govern the people. Governments exist in spheres of human responsibility, for instance, God ruled Israel through King David, but also through various elders, priests, and fathers/parents who were the citizens.[60]

In the same way, God is ruling through Nigerian politicians whether they have the fear of God or not. They are God's servants to execute God's will in

---

57. Oyediran, 35.
58. Chaplin, "Government," 415.
59. Chaplin, 416.
60. Kunhiyop, *African Christian Ethics*, 118.

the area he has assigned their governance. Every government official should be conscious of this divine nature of politics. It is not for self-aggrandizement but for the service of the people. Therefore, integrity of those who govern is a mandate. Acting as God's servants is not only about gaining political power or position, but about helping men and women of integrity in various political offices, preparing younger people for politics to take their places in the near future, and liberating communities from political jingoism or oppression.[61]

Thus, Nigerian democratic politics should not be about grasping or maintaining power, but making those in power use their position for the good of the entire society. It is about salvaging the masses and giving the people the best. Government with integrity does not come about on effort alone. It comes only when those in governance have a good and sound moral vision for their land and people. It comes only when political leaders have long-seated, well-researched, tested agendas for their nation's welfare and not their personal gratification.[62] It comes also when those in government have the fear of God and love for their country.

According to the Bible, the government acting as servants of God has the quality of not being partial in judgment, but judging fairly between all peoples, whether they are citizens or foreigners in the country, and hearing the small and great, the poor and rich alike. Governing with integrity means not yielding to the fear of man (Deut 1:16–18).[63] Justice and peace are the yardstick of government that serves with integrity. Such a government sacrifices the desires of the self for the desires of the people it governs.

When integrity is on the throne, the priority of those governing is not in multiplying cars, wives, silver and gold, and houses for themselves (Deut 17:16–17), nor lifting themselves above their fellow countrymen and women, but dividing the wealth of the land equally to every sector of the society. Integrity is good governance that recognizes and glorifies God and governs according to the commands of God and the national constitution. To walk in integrity, therefore, those who govern must give their time, energy, resources, and even their lives for the governed and not vice versa. As servant leaders and good shepherds of the citizens, those that govern should display their moral integrity by being ready to give up their lives for the sake of those they govern. Such leaders in government are also committed to the equal sharing of the wealth of the land with the communities and citizens they govern, rather than saving it

---

61. Yamsat, *Role of the Church*, 32.
62. Yamsat, 33.
63. Yamsat, 34.

for themselves in private bank accounts overseas, which they themselves may not ultimately use for the rest of their lives.[64] Therefore, to increase integrity in Nigerian democratic politics, the government must exercise their God-given abilities in their work. It is a matter of choice by those that govern the nation.

Governance as Public Servants

Those who are involved in public service are known as civil servants or public servants and they are also part of government. Politics is only one aspect of public service. The civil, military and paramilitary, police, and others, working in any government establishment, are part of the Nigerian government that needs to imbibe moral integrity. Compared to the private sector, public service is usually low in pay and benefits. Nevertheless, civil servants are expected to carry out their services with all honesty and contentment.[65]

Integrity includes honesty in public service. It is an opportunity to serve the people directly. The proper motivation for it should simply be the provision of service. That being the case, those who are not eager to use the opportunities provided by public service for personal gain, are the ones best suited for such services. These are the public servants that will promote government integrity. They should be God-fearing people, who depend on God for their provision. Because civil servants are really working for God and not for humans, those in public service should not need inducements to provide good services.[66] Integrity demands carefulness in doing what is right to all men and women at all times, so that they do not offend their Creator – the one they really seek to serve.

John the Baptist outlined two important qualities that are necessary to be an effective civil servant. When the tax collectors asked John what they should do, John replied, "Collect no more than what you have been ordered to" (Luke 3:13). To the soldiers who asked what they should do, John responded, "Do not take money from anyone by force, or accuse anyone falsely" (Luke 3:14). These two groups of public servants were addressed; there was one problem with two different manifestations. Tax collectors throughout history have had a tendency to take their share of the taxes on top of that which was demanded by government. It is wrong for civil servants to force people to pay extra on top of their taxes before receiving a proper tax clearance form. It is

---

64. Yamsat, 35.
65. Ozodo, *Nigerian Covenant*, 69.
66. Ozodo, 70.

also wrong for any government employer to extort money from an employee before giving employment. Soldiers are equally notorious for extortion, but they are even more dangerous because they carry arms. It is immoral and cowardly for soldiers and policemen to intimidate unarmed innocent civilians and demand that they provide them with *kola*. If it was wrong in the days of John the Baptist, it is wrong today, especially for Nigerian police.[67] Dozens of innocent citizens have been killed because they refused to give money to the police at checkpoints. The current "#end SARS"[68] protest by Nigerian youths testifies to the brutality of Nigerian soldiers and policemen.

There is so much corruption in public service. Extortion, bribery, and stealing are considered normal. Anyone who chooses to live by personal integrity is swimming against the tide and such public servants often suffer greatly. However, the Bible deals with such problems by reminding us that suffering for what is right is to be expected for every righteous person (2 Tim 3:12; 1 Pet 2:18–21; 4:12–16). It is a privilege to suffer for doing the right thing.[69] Public servants should, despite all odds, still regard honesty and integrity as their best policy.

Integrity includes contentment in public service. A second quality that is necessary to be an effective civil servant with godly integrity, was something else Jesus said to the soldiers – "be content with your wages" (Luke 3:14). Having a love for material things is one of the major reasons why soldiers and other civil servants try to extort money.[70] The solution to this problem is for the public servants to live by faith, trusting God to supply all their needs (Phil 4:19). Testimonies abound of people who have sought to please God before their own individual needs and who have had their needs supernaturally supplied. Paul writes:

> I have learned to be content in whatever circumstances I am. I know how to get along with humble means, and I also know how to live in prosperity; . . . I have learned the secret of being filled and going hungry, both of having abundance and suffering need. I can do all things through him who strengthens me. (Phil 4:11–13 NASB)

---

67. Ozodo, 70.
68. "#end SARS" means end or stop the activities of Special Anti-Robbery Squad (SARS).
69. Ozodo, *Nigerian Covenant*, 70.
70. Ozodo, 70.

Most government employees know that the pay for civil servants is mediocre. If a person cannot live on the salary and benefits paid by the government, he or she should seek to find other employment, instead of soiling the integrity of the government by his or her unethical behavior. Once you become a civil servant, the moral demand is that you must be content. However, to promote government integrity as public or civil servants, there is the need not only to serve but also to work for the total turn-around of Nigerians to ethical politics, governance, and public service.[71] This is one of the implications of being public servants. Public servants are employed to promote moral virtues and not moral vices. They are for the service of the nation and not to extort the public funds.

Public servants and the government in general should lead the way in promoting ethical standards and moral integrity. Those civil servants who still regard honesty as a high value should be commended and rewarded; the government should emulate Omega Bank, who instituted an annual award for the "Honest Person of Nigeria."[72] Ethical reorientation of civil servants is an integral part of the government's responsibility. The most practical way to restore moral values is to dress honest integrity in the cloths of motivation, rewarding those who exhibit honesty, integrity and sound moral values.[73]

Responsibility of the Electorates

The electorates are the bedrock of democratic politics. This is because democratic power rests with the people in any given society, and they are the people who delegate or entrust power to those who govern. In the Athenian form of democracy, citizens of the republic possessed power. Where there is division of opinion among the people, systems of voting determine the wishes of the majority in the society. Democratic traditions are therefore made up of a concept of power, which gives predominance to the people and to systems of political life which enable the wishes of the people to be carried out.[74]

"In all democratic thought, those who exercise power in the political forum do so as trustees on behalf of the democratic society. Governments [or political leaders] do not have either a divine, or any other, right to the unrestricted use of

---

71. Ozodo, 71.
72. Ibemere and Oduenyi, "Rewarding Honesty," 37.
73. Ibemere and Oduenyi, 37.
74. Gladwin, "Democracy," 294.

the power they possess."[75] Power belongs to the governed not the government. A democratic society needs a commitment to the fundamental social values of justice and equality. "If power is to rest with the people, the people need a sense of corporate identity and responsibility."[76] It is out of democratic ignorance that Nigerians feel that power belongs to those in authority.

The integrity of the electorates is important to call to account those who exercise power. "In democratic societies the people have mechanisms for removing from power those whom they have put there. In every truly democratic society, every government has to account to the people for its stewardship of the trust the people have placed in them."[77] There is negligence of integrity in Nigerian politics because the electorates do not know their rights as a democratic society. Therefore, instilling integrity in Nigerian politics has to begin with the people knowing their fundamental rights as a democratic society.

The Fundamental Rights of the Electorates

If integrity is to be revived in Nigerian politics, then the people of Nigeria have to accept the fundamental equality of all citizens as both created by God in his image and as being the object of his love in Christ, which the Christians in Nigeria proclaim.[78] The origin of people's rights is at creation; they are not "acquired," nor has any government or other authority conferred them. Every Nigerian citizen has them from the beginning. The citizens received their rights at birth from the hand of their maker. They are inherent in human creation. Stott puts it in another way: "Human rights are the rights of human beings, and the nature of human rights depends on the nature of the human beings, whose rights they are."[79] Fundamental, therefore to the people's rights is the question of what it means to be Nigerian. Thus, a truly democratic society with integrity affirms and upholds the dignity, the equality, of all, both before the law and in the responsibility of the exercise of political power. Therefore, to instill integrity in the life of the electorates, the people must do the following:

---

75. Gladwin, 294.
76. Gladwin, 294.
77. Gladwin, 295.
78. Gladwin, 295.
79. Stott, *Issues Facing Christians Today*, 154.

Affirm Our Human Dignity

The dignity of Nigeria as a democratic society of human beings is asserted in three successive sentences in Genesis 1:27–28:

> So God created man in His own image, in the image of God He created him; male and female He created them. God blessed them; and God said to them, "Be fruitful and multiply, and fill the earth, and subdue it; and rule over the fish of the sea and over the birds of the sky, and over every living thing that moves on the earth."

The first assertion is that God created human beings, including Nigerians, in his own image. Second, God created them male and female, man and woman, boy and girl. Third, God blessed them and told them "to fill the earth, and subdue it." The dignity of a democratic society is here seen to consist of three unique relationships which God established for Nigerians by creation, which together constitute a large part of our "Nigerianness," which the fall (our sinful nature) distorted, but did not destroy.

The first is our *relationship to God*. Nigerians are God-like beings, created by his will, in his image. This divine image has no respect for tribal or religious beliefs. The divine image includes those rational, moral, and spiritual qualities, which separate Nigerians from the animals and relate us to God. In consequence, Nigerians can learn about God from Christian evangelists or teachers (it is a basic human right to hear the gospel, the message that motivated the early nationalists into seeking independence); come to know, love and serve him; live in conscious, humble dependence upon him; and understand his will and obey his commands.[80]

So then, all those democratic rights – the freedom to profess, practice, and propagate religion, the freedom of worship, of conscience, of thought and of speech – come under this first rubric of the Nigerian relationship to God. It is striking that even the aspirants of Islam and African Traditional Religion know this instinctively and refer to the "Supreme Being" from whom human rights are ultimately desired.

The second unique capacity of "*Nigerianness*" or nationalism concerns our *relationship to one another*. The God who made the different ethnic groups and brought us together as a nation is himself a social being, one God comprising three eternally distinct modes of personhood. He said, "Let us make man in our image" (Gen 1:26), and "It is not good for the man to be alone" (2:18). So God made man, male and female, and told them to procreate. Out of this

---
80. Stott, 154–155.

procreation come the different ethnic groups that make up Nigeria as a nation-state. Thus, sexuality is God's creation, marriage is God's institution, and human companionship is God's purpose.[81] Therefore, all those human freedoms – the sanctity of sex, marriage, and family; the right of peaceful assembly; and the right to receive respect, irrespective of our age, sex, tribes, status, religion or profession – come under this second rubric of the Nigerian relationship to each other.

Our third distinctive quality as Nigerians is *our relationship to the earth* and its creatures. God has given Nigerians dominion, with instructions to subdue and cultivate the fruitful earth and rule its creatures. So then, all those democratic rights – the right to work and the right to rest; the right to share in the earth's resources; the right to food, clothing and shelter; the right to life and health and to their preservation; the right to freedom from poverty, hunger and disease – come under this third rubric of our relationship to the earth.[82] They are meant for the good of Nigerians and not for us to kill ourselves because of these natural resources.

Thus all the fundamental rights of a democratic society are foundational to the right to be human, and so to enjoy the dignity of having been created in God's image and of possessing in consequence unique relationships to God, to our fellow Nigerians and to the material world. In other words, our moral integrity in politics will improve as we relate to God in right worship, to fellow Nigerians in right fellowship, and to our natural resources in right stewardship.

Affirm Our Human Equality

The tragedy is that "democratic societal rights" have not always meant "equal rights." The good gifts of the Creator are spoiled by our own selfishness. The rights God gives to all Nigerians equally easily degenerate into "personal or individual" rights on which such individuals insist, irrespective of the rights of others or of the common good of the society. So the history of Nigerian politics has been the story of conflict between "my right and yours," between the good of each and the good of all, between the individual and the community, between one ethnic group and the others. Indeed, it is when democratic rights are in conflict with one another that the democratic society is presented with a difficult ethical dilemma.[83] Integrity of the electorates or a democratic society

---

81. Stott, 155.
82. Stott, 155.
83. Stott, 156–157.

means equal access to society's opportunities and privileges by all Nigerians. It means subjecting the rights of individuals to the greatest good of the society.[84]

The biblical emphasis on equal rights is that no powerful individuals may impose their will on the community, that no community or majority violates the rights of an individual or minority. The Mosaic law carefully protected the weak and vulnerable. "Far from exploiting them, God's people were to be the voice of the voiceless and the champion of the powerless."[85] The biblical injunction is that a democratic society must show "no partiality" (Deut 1:16–17) in its attitude to political leaders or politicians, and give no special defense to some because they are rich, favored, or influential. The biblical writers insisted on this. Moses declared: "The LORD your God is God of gods and Lord of lords, the great, the mighty, the awesome God, who does not show partiality . . ." (Deut 10:17 NASB). Therefore, Israelites were to show no partiality either, but rather give justice to "the small and the great alike" (Deut 1:17 NASB).

The same emphasis occurs in the New Testament. God is the impartial judge. He does not regard external appearances or circumstances. He shows no favoritism, whatever our racial, tribal, or social background may be (see Acts 10:34; Rom 2:11; 1 Pet 1:17).[86] Perhaps in flattery, but still with accuracy, Jesus Christ was described in these terms: "Teacher, we know that you are a man of integrity. You aren't swayed by others, because you pay no attention to who they are" (Mark 12:14). In other words, Jesus neither defers to the rich and powerful, nor despises the poor and weak, but gives equal respect to all, whatever their social status. A democratic society like Nigeria must do the same.

All Nigerians have equal rights because they have the same Creator. Both the dignity and the equality of their "Nigerianness" are traced in Scripture to their unique creation.[87] The common humanity is enough to abolish favoritism and privilege, and to establish equal status and rights in Nigerian politics.

Affirm Our Human Responsibility

The citizens in a democratic society have *duties and responsibilities as well as rights*. The civilization that Nigeria embraces, has had a sweeping away of duties and an expansion of rights. There has been much emphasis on the human rights of the citizens with little or no mention of their responsibilities.[88] But

---

84. Ozodo, *Nigerian Covenant*, 49–50.
85. Stott, *Issues Facing Christians Today*, 157.
86. Stott, 158.
87. Stott, 158.
88. Stott, 159.

we have two lungs. No human being can manage to breathe with one lung and not with the other. In the same way, a democratic society must avail itself of rights and duties in equal measure.

The Christian Bible says much about defending other people's rights, but little about defending one's own. On the contrary, when it addresses us, it emphasizes our responsibilities, not our rights. The individuals in society are to love God and to love their neighbors. These primary requirements comprise the democratic society's whole duty; for, according to Jesus, "all the Law and the Prophets hang on these two commandments" (Matt 22:40). In fact, the Bible contains a universal declaration of responsibilities of a democratic society (especially in terms of loving God and neighbor), not of human rights. Thus, to instill integrity in Nigerian politics, democratic society must affirm human responsibility. Because God has laid it upon individuals to love and serve their neighbor, therefore we must fight for their rights, while being ready to renounce our own in order to do so. That is integrity in a democratic society. The individuals have to accept that other people's rights are their responsibility.[89]

In the process of nation building, therefore, individuals who have distinguished themselves by their performances should be acclaimed and honored in a democratic society. It is the responsibility of a democratic society that issues of great national concern must be subjected to rigorous public debates and criticism in order to arrive at a consensus, without undue delay in making progress. It is their duty to avoid obstinate confrontation because it undermines working relationships, cooperative activities, and mutual understanding; it places stumbling blocks in the path of peace, stability, security, and unity; and it retards genuine progress and achievements. It is the responsibility of a democratic society to regard and treat contestants as "opponents," and not as "enemies" that deserve not to live.[90]

In a democratic society, responsibility implies that every ethnic group has equal advantage in the control of power and sharing of amenities. All the ethnic groups in Nigeria should have the dignity, equality, and responsibility to be involved in mainstream Nigerian politics. Ethnic differences should not be a disadvantage in the control of political power. It is also the duty of a democratic society to fight against illiteracy and ignorance in society because they are obstacles to social, economic, cultural, political, scientific, and technological

---

89. Stott, 160–161.
90. Dzurgba, *Nigerian Politics and Moral Behaviour*, 72.

developments. Perpetuation of illiteracy and ignorance by social policies and political strategies should be rejected in a democratic society.[91]

In Nigerian democratic politics, all citizens should be informed of their obligations and responsibilities to the society and the government. The citizens should be made to understand that one of the dangerous brands of poverty is the poverty of moral character. They should be encouraged to strive continually to improve their moral integrity in their social life, places of work, and voting behavior. In the interest of healthy politics, a democratic society should encourage its citizens to *be* right and to *do* right, whether their motives and actions are properly understood and appreciated or not. Every opportunity should be utilized to put democracy into practice through the honest nomination of candidates, election hustings, and actual voting during elections. The struggle for the control of political power should not be done purely on the grounds of controlling the societal economy. Rather it should be done so as to promote the well-being of the democratic society. The end of politics should be the welfare of all Nigerians.[92] To boost the political image of the nation, a democratic society should adopt the principle of "live and let others live" because of our pluralistic nature.

Enhancement of Public Opinion

To revive moral integrity in Nigerian politics, the *intellectuals* in society need to review their political theory and activity. The concept of public opinion with regard to politics must be ethically evaluated; there needs to be serious reflection on the citizens' philosophy of politics. Democratic principles within the Nigerian context must be clearly defined and strengthened. A political cadre that implies that whatever is legally permissible cannot be morally wrong, and that what is morally wrong is a matter of public indifference, poses a serious threat to our democratic society. Nigerian intellectuals have a task of civic renewal, not just to repel democracy's assailants,[93] but they must fight to restore and build unique democratic foundations in Nigerian politics. This requires comprehensive effort. The connective tissue of Nigeria as a nation is neither democracy nor information or education. Every Nigerian citizen must indeed have some understanding of democratic political processes – male

---

91. Dzurgba, 73.
92. Dzurgba, 73.
93. Henry, *Has Democracy Had Its Day?*, 46.

or female, young or old – all must contribute in some personal way to the advancement of truth, love, integrity, and justice in the nation.

The moral issues being raised today in Nigerian governance are not focused just on the margins of politics; the whole political enterprise is being cross-examined anew in the context of ethics or morality. Justice and truth, for example, are not merely matters of tolerance, especially not tolerance of evil or unrighteousness. A revival of healthy democratic politics in Nigeria requires a clear voting majority (not an ethnic or religious majority), and, more importantly, a shared moral vision and purpose championed especially by the intellectuals.[94]

Who are these "intellectuals" in Nigeria? The intellectuals are the sages, the learners, the philosophers, and truth searchers who have rational reasoning and possess a mental quotient possibly superior to that of the average Nigerian on the street. On a serious note, Nigerian intellectuals have generally shirked their traditional responsibility of searching for and exposing the truth and directing the polity as appropriate in Nigerian politics. The Nigerian intellectual elites ought to propel integrity in politics because they are the elites – the political philosophers, people who reason, sages, and knowledgeable people in a democratic society. Common to the intellectuals is a desire for truth, a taste for advanced knowledge, a great mental ability, and the constant search for truth and justice. They are the conscience and moral custodian of the democratic society in which they live.[95]

Therefore, to imbibe moral and political integrity into democratic society in Nigeria, the intellectual elites have to affirm the individuals and their corporate responsibility. Their contributions to Nigerian democratic politics are very valid. The ideas they would generate and their criticisms of the affairs in the democratic society could be more effective than the daily policy actions of those in government. The intellectual elites are also the principal medium through which the human resources necessary for positive development are produced. They have what it takes to strive constantly and in all circumstances – whether under a despotic or democratic political leader – to guide against and monitor the foibles of the democratic society, most especially the excesses of those in political authority. These sages should do this through the objective, truthful, and responsible criticism of public issues, without fear or favor, and in a manner that avoids setting the nation ablaze. Tenaciously, they cling to the path of truth and moral rectitude. Thus, the intellectuals in Nigeria are

---

94. Henry, 46.
95. Sani, "Intellectual in Nation-Building," 126–127.

strategically placed and can be either lubricants or corrosive agents in the complex machinery of national political and moral integrity.[96]

Therefore, let the Nigerian intellectual elites take up their positions in the democratic society to affirm their sincere patriotism and idealism without compromise on principles. They should rise up to their calling, and should not join the ranks of exploiters while appointed as government functionaries. They should stop fighting between themselves or acquiescing by keeping quiet in the face of oppression in the society. The intellectual elites should join the catalytic vanguard of revolutionary transformation in Nigerian democratic politics along with the sprawling, underprivileged masses of the democratic society.[97] A radical revolution will come about when there is a transformation of political attitudes on the part of intellectuals, and a corresponding transformation of roles along with progressive forces in our democratic society. That will be a meaningful contribution to the process of reviving integrity in Nigerian politics.

Nigeria needs more people like Dr. Mrs. Ngozi Okonji-Iweala, an economist and international development expert, who had a twenty-five-year career at the World Bank in Washington DC as a development economist and rose to the ranks of the number two position of Managing Director of Operations (she is currently nominated as Director General). She was born in Ogwashi-Ukwu, Delta State, Nigeria, and was the first woman to hold the position of Nigeria's Finance Minister and Minister of Foreign Affairs. During her first term as Finance Minister under President Obasanjo's administration, she spearheaded negotiations with the Paris Club of Creditors that led to the cancellation of USD $30 billion of Nigeria's debt, as well as the outright cancellation of $18 billion from the International Monetary Fund.[98]

In 2003, Okonji-Iweala led efforts to improve Nigeria's macroeconomic management including the implementation of an oil-price-based fiscal rule where revenues accruing above a reference benchmark oil price were saved in a special account, "The Excess Crude Account," which helped to reduce macroeconomic volatility. She also introduced the practice of publishing each state's monthly financial allocation from the Federal Government. Finally, she helped build an electronic financial management platform – the Government Integrated Financial Management and Information System (GIFMIS), including

---

96. Sani, 126–127.
97. Sani, 130.
98. International Centre for Investigative Reporting, 9 Apr 2018, https://www.icirnigeria.org/another-looters-list-okonjo-iweala-writes-book-on-corrupt-and-vested-interests/; *Africa Focus Bulletin*, 27 Oct 2005, http://www.africafocus.org/docs05/nig0510.php.

the Treasury Single Account (TSA) and the Integrated Payroll and Personnel Information System (IPPIS) – helping to curtail corruption in the process. The IPPIS platform eliminated a lot of ghost workers from the system and saved the Nigerian government billions of US dollars in the process. Nigeria will not forget the effort of this woman who seemed to be too holy for Nigerian politics.

Christians and Nigerian Politics

The Christian community has what it takes to bring moral integrity into Nigerian politics through its teachings and involvement. In the past, Nigeria has been a revolution of blood-shedding politics. But Christians, as citizens, have the divine mandate to turn the country's democratic politics into a politics of morality and ethical behavior. Even though we believe the Lord to be God of all peoples, God has a special relationship with the Christians in any society.[99] God's sovereign choice of Christians, who are the "new Israel," is a privilege that involves a responsibility. Nigerian Christians today are also part of the "new Israel." Thus, what God said through Amos to Israel of old is directly to Christians in Nigeria today: "You only have I chosen among all the families of the earth" (Amos 3:2).[100] In other words, God is saying that, "of all the families in Nigeria, the Christians only have I known." God loves all Nigerians but he has a unique relationship with the Christians. Therefore, God places Christians under a solemn obligation to serve him faithfully in a democratic society.[101]

A Christian is a citizen of two worlds, the temporal and the eternal.[102] As citizens of Nigeria, Christians must take their citizenship very seriously. Citizenship for Christians involves applying the insights and principles of biblical faith into Nigerian politics – with its local, state, national, international, and even global structures – through responsible, active participation in the political process. This means that they must act responsibly in shaping the moral character of the democratic society in which they live. Citizenship demands understanding and participation; responsible citizens are the ones who understand the way their groups are structured in order to make corporate decisions, and thereby create public policy, establish social systems, and allocate resources. Christians must also participate in decision-making and course charting. In other words, Christian authentic citizenship demands both

---

99. Aghawenu, *A Call for Divine Justice*, 48.
100. Aghawenu, 48.
101. Aghawenu, 49.
102. Barnette, *Introducing Christian Ethics*, 172.

understanding *and* participation. The citizenship of Christians is important for shaping and leading democratic societies towards peace, justice, compassion, truth, integrity, and the whole panoply of ethical values which are totally at home under the roof of biblical righteousness.[103]

Citizenship is a corporate activity, just as Christian discipleship is a corporate experience, not just in the sense of the disciple being in relationship to the Master, but in the sense of the disciple being in relationship with others. Jesus said, "By this everyone will know that you are my disciples, if you love one another" (John 13:35). Being a Christian does not alienate one from being a Nigerian. Citizenship is a way we express our oneness as Nigerians. Thus, as Nigerian Christians work in the political process to accomplish good things for their fellow Nigerians, they are putting into action the biblical call to community.[104]

It is a biblical mandate as citizens of Nigeria to use our corporate resources to help those in need and to help bring about the highest ethical standards. The Nigerian system of government has been fashioned with both of these objectives in mind. Therefore, as Christians walk through the political process to be a voice for the needy (who are usually a people without much of a voice), and as they work to create a moral, just, and peaceful democratic society, they are engaging in actions that are not simply political and humanitarian, but powerfully spiritual.[105]

To improve the moral status of national politics, citizens of Nigeria need to demand education in biblical thought, education on various issues, and education on political processes, based on the synthesis of pertinent information. Involvement in politics is the "proof of the pudding." There are many ways and many levels in which Christians can become responsibly involved. William H. Elder articulated some vital political areas that Christians can be involved in as citizens of any nation such as voting in elections, lobbying, campaigning, joining coalitions and groups, and running for political office.[106] These are some of the political processes in which Christians in Nigeria ought to be involved in order to shape the nation in the light of biblical integrity.

Voting in elections fulfils the barest minimum involvement in the political process, that is, to vote for the Conservative candidate or the Democratic Party. To improve the system, Christians in Nigeria should be involved so much

---

103. Elder, "Politics and Christian Discipleship," 123.
104. Elder, 135.
105. Elder, 138.
106. Elder, 138–143.

more in aggressive study and analysis, communication with office holders, lobbying or influencing politicians on a particular issue, or persuading them to support or oppose a change in the law. According to Elder, "expressing one's view can be done through letters, postcards, petitions, phone calls, and personal visits."[107] *Lobbying and campaigning* can be done through social media platforms and communication technology. Christians can lead a campaign or take part in planned activities, using positive and dynamic manners without abusive language, that are intended to achieve a particular social, commercial, or political change or in order to win an election.

Coalition building is also vital if Christians are to inculcate integrity in Nigerian politics. There is nothing wrong for Christians to form a coalition, which is "a group formed by people from several different groups, especially political ones, agreeing to work together for a particular purpose."[108] Christians' involvement in political coalitions and groups can influence manifestos and policies by integrating biblical norms into the political processes.

Finally, Christians are at liberty to fully *run for any office* of their choice in every level and function of government. "Christian people who understand the process, who want to serve rather than rule, who love their nation but refuse to worship it, who can handle power well and do not need it to fill some ego void, who want to fashion a just and compassionate and free society for all people, who will do what is right rather than what is expedient or what feathers their own nest, are desperately needed in all levels of government across our nation and around our world."[109]

To sum up, instilling integrity through our Christian teaching means applying the gospel of our Lord Jesus Christ, under the leadership of the Holy Spirit, to our Nigerian governance through responsible involvement in the political process. As citizens of Nigeria, Christians have every right to be fully involved in every level and function of democratic government. According to biblical injunctions, Christians have every responsibility to be actively involved in shaping our country, in the light of God's will for it. Christian involvement is a mandate as a citizen, not an option, for all who take seriously their call to discipleship by our Redeemer and Lord Jesus Christ.

---

107. Elder, 141.
108. "Coalition," *Oxford Advance Learner's Dictionary*, 283.
109. Elder, "Politics and Christian Discipleship," 143.

7

The Way Forward in Nigerian Politics

A word of summary is now necessary in order to bring this study to a close. The enormous moral bankruptcy in Nigerian democratic politics is of great concern. Thus, we attempt to proffer a solution based on the perspective of biblical Christianity, that is, to apply the biblical revelation regarding politics and ethics to this vital issue of integrity in Nigerian politics. In other words, to use the normative ethic of politics as revealed in the Bible to unravel the problem of moral failure in Nigerian governance and establish that integrity as a moral venture is essential to Nigerian government.

The first objective of the study was to expose the Nigerian democratic society, political stalwarts, and government to the biblical concepts of ethics, politics, and integrity and this was achieved in chapter 1. The study developed the biblical overview of the significance of integrity in Israel's politics. Here, the work disclosed the origin of politics – that it originated from the very heart of God and was entrusted to humanity right from creation. Israel as a nation was chosen to model integrity in human governance but it failed, as disclosed in the Old Testament. In the New Testament God elected the "new Israel," the church, to proffer the moral nature of God on earth. Thus, the concept of integrity was fully developed. Integrity was defined as the quality or state of being of sound moral principles, uprightness, honesty, and sincerity. Some characteristics of integrity were also discussed based on biblical revelation.

This study also disclosed the adverse effects of moral bankruptcy in Nigerian democratic politics through the x-rays of ecology and practice of Nigerian political society. Some of the causes of the lack of integrity were disclosed, which are a poor understanding of politics and democracy, a lack of ideological basis for party formation, manipulation of ethnic or religious sentiments, imposition of power by the political elites, false nationalism and patriotism in governance, the inability to accept losing an election, a lust of materialism, and the nonchalant attitude of Christians to politics. The effects of the lack of integrity were also discussed. These were identified as political instability and national disintegration, the emergence of political "god-fathers," the suppression of human rights and values, government delay tactics, and the emergence of rich politicians in the midst of poverty.

The book further discussed how to administer, revive, or instill integrity into Nigerian politics. The biblical exposition of integrity was applied to some specific areas such as the politicians, the political parties, the Nigerian government, the electorates, and the Christian faith. It was disclosed that integrity is a two-way road, including both righteousness and justice. That is, it is a right relationship with God *and* a right relationship with our fellow human beings. Living right with God is righteousness, and living right with our neighbors is justice. Thus, becoming a person of integrity has to do with *who* we are and *what* we do. This study, therefore, highlighted the causes and effects of moral failure in Nigerian democratic politics and presented biblical teachings on moral integrity as useful tools to improve the political situation in the country. It is hoped that every citizen of this great nation will abide by the principles disclosed in this book in order to boost the integrity of Nigerian politics.

Having dealt with the place of integrity in Nigerian democratic politics, the following suggestions and recommendations will be given for an effective result and for future study on Christian political ethics.

New Orientation on the Political Process

Nigerians need education on what democratic politics is all about. This assessment of the Nigerian political experience shows that the Nigerian democratic transition has been truncated by a wrong concept of politics. Democratic politics, which is meant for the common good of the citizens, has gradually given way to personal aggrandizement as individuals turn their fiefdoms into gardens where they can personally flourish.[1] The result is that Nigerians are alienated and have to fend for themselves, and the bureaucracy suffers a psychological dent.

To actualize the Nigeria of our dreams, that is, a nation that is just, caring, and democratic, our political orientation has to change. "The search

---

1. Kukah, *Democracy and Civil Society in Nigeria*, xvii.

for this ideal is not a quixotic excursion into the sunset of blind idealism and unguarded ambition."[2] The national political orientation must be anchored on the belief that Nigeria is one "big road between the Jericho of fear and anxiety and the promise of a Jerusalem of peace, justice and love. In between, there are . . . rocks inhabited by dangerous charlatans."[3] On this road, the citizens of Nigeria must beg for eyes to enable them to discern between virtue and vice, freedom and slavery, justice and injustice, right and wrong, love and hatred, and nationalism and tribalism, all to the glory of God who unites the various ethnic groups into one great nation called Nigeria.

Dr. Nnamdi Azikiwe's political philosophy is vital at this time to promote democratic politics in Nigeria. Azikiwe believed that the philosophical ideal is a state where Nigeria and the rest of Africa would be divorced from ethnic affiliations and traditional authorities and transformed by five pillars: spiritual balance, social regeneration, economic determinism, and mental emancipation and "Risorgimento" nationalism.[4] Azikiwe was a statesman who was the first President of Nigeria Republic. "Considered a driving force behind the nation's independence, he came to be known as the 'father of Nigerian Nationalism.'"[5] Nigerian politicians have a lot to learn from Azikiwe political philosophy.

Godly Leadership in Nigerian Politics

What John Stott writes in his book, *Issues Facing Christians Today*, about "a serious dearth of good leaders" in the Western world is applicable in contemporary Nigerian democratic politics; thus his thoughts influence this section – Godly Leadership in Nigerian Politics. Citizens feel confused, bewildered, and alienated. To borrow the metaphors of Jesus, Nigerians seem to be like "sheep without a shepherd," while our political leaders often appear to be "blind leaders of the blind." "There is a great need . . . for more clear-sighted, courageous, and dedicated leaders."[6] For an evolution of a vibrant integrity in our democratic politics, there is urgent need of godly men and women in leadership positions.

Nigeria needs *visionary* leaders in governance. Men and women who will not gamble with their moral lives, or be satisfied with the political status quo

---

2. Kukah, 280.
3. Kukah, 280.
4. Wikipedia, "Nnamdi Azikiwe."
5. Wikipedia, "Nnamdi Azikiwe."
6. Stott, *Issues Facing Christians Today*, 486.

of the nation. Leaders who have a deep dissatisfaction with what is and a clear vision of what could be. "It begins with indignation over the status quo and it grows into the earnest quest for an alternative"[7] that will boost the moral image of Nigeria.[8] Godly leaders with vision, program their minds with positive and constructive desires, imagination, and expectations that will help to move Nigeria forward.

Nigeria needs godly leaders that are *industrious*. Godly leaders are people with a creative imagination wedded to an indomitable industry. Therefore, to promote and to protect integrity in Nigerian politics, vision and reality, passion and practicality, must go together and be visible in godly leadership.[9]

Nigeria needs godly leaders that *persevere* in order for democratic politics to succeed and thrive; indeed, perseverance is an indispensable quality. A man or woman of integrity will stand firm even when opposition comes, which is bound to happen. As soon as the campaign for integrity in politics "gets under way, the forces of reaction muster, entrenched privilege digs itself in more deeply, commercial interests feel threatened and raise the alarm, the cynical sneer at the folly of 'do-gooders,' and apathy transmute[s] into hostility."[10]

But a true leadership with the *fear of God* thrives on opposition. "Its silver is refined and its steel hardened."[11] Godly leaders have "resilience to take setbacks in their stride, the tenacity to overcome fatigue and discouragement, and the wisdom to turn 'stumbling blocks into stepping-stones.'"[12] The leaders that will promote integrity in Nigerian democratic politics must be "palpably single-minded and unselfish-seeking. They must be strong enough to face opposition and ridicule, staunch enough to endure obstruction and delay."[13] These are the qualities Nigerian leaders must possess in abundance. However, godly "leaders are not impervious to criticism." Rather, "they listen to it and weigh it, and may modify their program accordingly." But such leaders "do not waver in their basic conviction of what God has called them to do" for their beloved nation. "Whatever the opposition aroused or the sacrifice entailed, the godly leaders

---

7. Stott, 487.
8. Stott, 487.
9. Aghawenu, *Ministerial Ethics*, 48.
10. Stott, *Issues Facing Christians Today*, 491.
11. Stott, 491.
12. Stott, 491.
13. Stott, 492.

persevere."[14] Thus for a stubborn integrity in Nigerian politics, there must be the grace of perseverance in leadership.

A godly leadership demand in Nigerian politics is a service to Nigeria. The servant leadership model was introduced by Jesus into the world (Mark 10:42–45). Godly leadership is not a synonym for lordship. Thus Nigerian leaders are called into governance to be servants not bosses, slaves not masters. In other words, the emphasis is not on the authority of a ruler-leader but on the humility of leadership. That is, "the authority by which the Christian leader leads is not power but love, not force but example, not coercion but reasoned persuasion. Leaders have power, but power is safe only in the hands of those who humble themselves to serve."[15] This is a tacit recognition of the intrinsic worth of all Nigerians.

Finally, the final mark of integrity in godly leadership is *discipline*. Not self-discipline in general, such as in the mastery of one's passion, time and energies, but in particular the discipline with which a leader waits on God for strength and direction. Political leaders should know their weaknesses. They know the greatness of political positions and the strength of the opposition. But godly leaders must also know the inexhaustible riches of God's grace. In other words, godly leaders discipline themselves in prayer and lead the nation to pray as well. "It is only those who discipline themselves to seek God's face who keep their vision and integrity bright."[16]

In summary, Nigeria needs godly, hard-working leaders with clear vision, dogged perseverance, humble service, and iron discipline,[17] in order to boost the integrity in Nigerian democratic politics. We need to learn from our past leaders like Dr. Alex Ekwueme, for instance, who served as vice-president of Nigeria from 1979 to 1983 under President Shehu Shagari. Before Dr. Ekwueme gained national and international attention as the vice-president, he was actively involved in socio-economic development of his community. He started an active Educational Trust Fund that has been responsible for sponsoring the education of several hundred youths to universities in Nigeria and abroad.

Dr. Ekwueme was a member of the housing sub-committee of Adebo Salaries and Wages Review Commission. He also served for many years on the board of the Anambra State Housing Development Authority on the national

---

14. Stott, 493.
15. Stott, 494.
16. Stott, 497.
17. Aghawenu, *Ministerial Ethics*, 49.

front. He participated as well in the Nigeria National Constitutional Conference (NCC) in Abuja, where he served on the committee on the Structure and Framework of the Constitution. His famous proposal at the NCC for just and equitable power-sharing in Nigeria based on the six geopolitical zones has now come to be accepted as necessary for maintaining a stable Nigerian polity. He mobilized thirty-four eminent Nigerians who risked their lives to stand up against General Sani Abacha's dictatorship during the era of military politics in Nigeria. He was a patriotic godly leader our politicians should emulate – a philanthropist, public servant, and a man of peace.

Theocentric Approach to Political Life

The foundation of integrity in the political process is not rules but the changeless character of God. The Bible portrays God as the Creator of all things perfect, preceding and superseding all things. It also emphasizes how human beings are originally created to emulate God. This changeless character of God ought to be reflected in any human governance. Therefore, three divine characteristics of God are essential for moral up-keeping in political activities. The essentials are the *holiness* of God, the *justice* of God, and the *loveliness* of God. Nigerian politics will be transformed if it reflects God's holy-just-loving character.[18]

Holiness is a call to Nigeria to zealously make God their highest priority, and following that, is zeal for God in politics. Holiness calls for purity in all political processes, reflecting God's moral perfection and separation from all manner of political vices. Holiness also holds citizens accountable by rewarding moral purity, by infusing integrity into the political processes, and by punishing impurity and dishonesty. Finally holiness calls citizens of Nigeria to a valley of humility, which is the natural outcome of seeking to imitate God's holiness.[19]

A just God demands *justice* in democratic politics. The concept of the rights of all citizens is central to justice. By virtue of being God's image bearers (Gen 1:27), all Nigerians have been endowed with two fundamental rights: the right to be treated with dignity, and the right to exercise free will, as mentioned earlier in this study. The biblical injunction is to follow "justice, and only justice" (Deut 16:20). Justice demands procedural rights, which focus on fair processes in decision-making in politics and other wise. It demands equal protection: "You shall do no injustice in judgment; you shall not be partial to the poor nor defer to the great, but you are to judge your neighbor

---

18. Hill, *Just Business*, 15.
19. Hill, 27.

fairly" (Lev 19:15). True justice in the political process is blind, particularly in regard to race, tribe, religion, class, and socio-economic status. Political justice for all in voting, electing, lobbying, and campaigning is the demand in Nigerian politics.

A loving God, who ordained Nigeria as a nation-state, demands a loving political relationship irrespective of political party affiliation. Love should be the centerpiece of democratic governance. This is a divine love characterized by empathy, mercy, and self-sacrifice. It is true that successful political hustling depends more on cooperation than competition. But without a loving and solid relational foundation, no corporate effort in politics can succeed in the longterm.[20]

In sum, to boost integrity in the Nigerian democratic government, there is need for a God-centered political process that is characterized by divine holiness, justice, and love to be respected equally by all Nigerians. This theocentric approach in Nigerian politics moves beyond both consequences and moral rules, aspiring for nothing less than God-like behavior.[21] It is a quest for Nigeria to imitate God.

Finally, being exposed to a sound biblical concept of integrity in Nigerian politics does not automatically solve the problem of moral bankruptcy. No matter how reliable the exposition or how gifted the researcher, the declaration of truth does not provide the removal of the moral issue. The Bible is normative and authoritative; it is also clear and direct.[22] There is no magic in the Bible passages that automatically brings solutions into the neglect of integrity by way of a magic carpet. The solution comes by application, by learning how to handle those inevitable conflicts or issues in the political process. God is the initiator and sustainer for achieving a quality, healthy, stable democratic political government in Nigeria. Therefore, Nigerians should depend on God as we pick-up this challenge to build and re-build the Nigeria of our dreams, where peace, unity, and justice shall reign to the envy of the rest of the world and to the glory of God.

---

20. Hill, 48.
21. Hill.
22. Aghawenu, *Ministerial Ethics*.

Bibliography

Abogunrin, S. O. "Religion and Democracy in Nigeria." *Orita: Ibadan Journal of Religious Studies* 31, no. 1–2 (1999): 1–18.

———. "Religion and Ethics." In *Religion and Ethics in Nigeria*, edited by S. O. Abogunrin. Ibadan Religious Studies Series Volume 1. Ibadan: Daystar Press, 1986.

Abubaka, D. "The Federal Character Principle, Consociationalism and Democratic Stability in Nigeria." In *Federalism and Political Restructuring in Nigeria*, edited by K. Amuwo et al., 164–176. Ibadan: Spectrum Books, repr. 2003.

Achebe, C. *The Trouble with Nigeria*. Enugu: Fourth Dimension Publishers, 1983.

Adamolekun, Taiye. "The Role of Religion in the Political and Ethical Re-Orientation of Nigeria." *Orita: Ibadan Journal of Religious Studies* 31, no. 1–2 (1999): 19–28.

Adebanjio, A. "The Inheritors" *TELL*. August 2, 1999, 3.

Adeleye, M. O. "Religion, Politics and Society." In *Religion and State: The Nigerian Experience*, edited by S. A. Adewale, 63–75. Ibadan: Orita Publications, 1988.

Adeniran, L. A. "Colonial Rule and Factors of Development in the Oyo North Area of Oyo State." In *Issues in Contemporary African Social and Political Thought*, volume 2, edited by O. Obafemi and B. Lawal, 18–23. Lagos: Academia Publications, 1994.

Adeyemo, W. "A Loud Family Quarrel." *TELL*, December 27, 2004, 16–23.

Agbodike, C. C. "Federal Character Principle and National Integration." *Federalism and Political Restructuring in Nigeria*, edited by K. Amuwo et al., 177–190. Ibadan: Spectrum Books, 2003.

Aghawenu, G. F. N. *A Call for Divine Justice*. Ojota-Lagos: Mongraphics, 2002.

———. *Ministerial Ethics*. Ojota-Lagos: Mongraphics, 2003.

Aina, A. D. *Party Politics in Nigeria under Obasanjo Administration*. Shomolu: Emaphine Reprographics, 2002.

Akao, J. O. "Christianity and the Quest for Democracy in Nigeria." *Orita: Ibadan Journal of Religious Studies* (1999): 53–58.

Albert, O. "Federalism, Inter-Ethnic Conflicts and the Northernisation Policy of the 1950s and 1960s." In *Federalism and Political Restructuring in Nigeria*, edited by K. Amuwo et al., 50–63. Ibadan: Spectrum Books, 2003.

Awolalu, J. O. "Religion and National Unity." In *Religion and National Unity*, edited by S. B. Mala, 2–6. Ibadan: Orita Publication, 1988.

———. "Religion and State." *Religion and State: The Nigerian Experience*, edited by S. A. Adewale, 8–12. Ibadan: Orita Publications, 1988.

Ayandele, E. A. *The Educated Elite in the Nigerian Society*. Ibadan: Ibadan University Press, 1974.

Ayantayo, J. K. "A Comparative Study of Eschatology in the Bible and the Qur'an from the Moral Perspective and Its Relevance for Today." *Ado Journal of Religious Studies* 1 (July 2002): 29–31.
Babarinsa, D. "The Unusual Gladiators." *TELL*, January 3, 2005.
Barnette, H. H. *Introducing Christian Ethics*. Nashville: Broadman Press, 1961.
———. "Protestants and Political Responsibility." *Review and Expositor* 65 (Summer 1968): 299.
Bauckham, R. J. "Politics." In *New Dictionary of Christian Ethics and Pastoral Theology*, edited by D. J. Atkinson, D. F. Field, A. F. Holmes, and O. O'Donovan, 669. Downers Grove: InterVarsity Press, 1995.
Birch, B. C., and L. L. Rasmussen. *Bible and Ethics in the Christian Life*. Minneapolis: Augsburg, 1989.
Blackaby, Richard, ed. *The Blackaby Study Bible*. Nashville: Thomas Nelson, 2006.
Bridger, F. W. "Trust." In *New Dictionary of Christian Ethics and Pastoral Theology*, edited by D. J. Atkinson, D. F. Field, A. F. Holmes, and O. O'Donovan, 866. Downers Grove: InterVarsity Press, 1995.
Bunting, I. D. "Poverty." In *New Dictionary of Christian Ethics and Pastoral Theology*, edited by D. J. Atkinson, D. F. Field, A. F. Holmes, and O. O'Donovan, 678. Downers Grove: InterVarsity Press, 1995.
Burns, A. *History of Nigeria*. London: George Allen & Unwin, 1958.
Chaplin, J. P. "Government." In *New Dictionary of Christian Ethics and Pastoral Theology*, edited by D. J. Atkinson, D. F. Field, A. F. Holmes, and O. O'Donovan, 415–417. Downers Grove: InterVarsity Press, 1995.
Cole, G. A. "Responsibility." In *New Dictionary of Christian Ethics and Pastoral Theology*, edited by D. J. Atkinson, D. F. Field, A. F. Holmes, and O. O'Donovan, 734–736. Downers Grove: InterVarsity Press, 1995.
Cowan, L. G. *The Dilemmas of African Independence*. New York: Walker & Co., 1968.
Diamond, L. *Class, Ethnicity and Democracy in Nigeria*. New York: Syracuse University Press, 1995.
Douglas, J. D., and J. C. Whitcomb. "Daniel." In *New Bible Dictionary*, edited by J. D. Douglas, N. Hillyer, and F. F. Bruce, 262. 2nd Edition. Leicester, UK: Inter-Varsity Press, 1982.
Durkheim, E. *The Elementary Forms of the Religious Life*. London: George Allen & Unwin, 1915. http://www.gutenberg.org/files/41360/41360-h/41360-h.htm#Page_445.
Dzurgba, A. *Nigerian Politics and Moral Behaviour*. Ibadan: John Archers, 2008.
———. *Principles of Ethics*. Ibadan: Agape Publications, 2000.
Eades, J. S. "Religion, Politics and Ideology." In *Religion and Society in Nigeria*, edited by J. K. Olupona and T. Falola, 181–187. Ibadan: Spectrum Books, 1991.
Egner, D. C. *Knowing God through Job*. The Bible in Perspective Series. Grand Rapids: Radio Bible Class, 1987.

Elder, W. H. "Politics and Christian Discipleship." In *Understanding Christian Ethics*, edited by W. M. Tillman Jr, 123–144. Nashville: B&H, 1998.
Ellison, H. I. "Job." In *New Bible Dictionary*, edited by J. D. Douglas, N. Hillyer, and F. F. Bruce. 2nd edition. Leicester, UK: Inter-Varsity Press, 1982.
Ero, A. "Presidency: Southern Leaders are Chasing Shadows." *TELL*. January 3, 2005, 18–19.
Ezera, K. *Constitutional Developments in Nigeria*. Cambridge: Cambridge University Press, 1964.
Fellow Country Men and Women: Great Maiden Speeches of the Nigerian Military in National Governance. Enugu: ABIC Books, 2004.
Fletcher, D. B. "Dehumanisation." In *New Dictionary of Christian Ethics and Pastoral Theology*, edited by D. J. Atkinson, D. F. Field, A. F. Holmes, and O. O'Donovan, 291. Downers Grove: InterVarsity Press, 1995.
Geisler, N. L. *Christian Ethics: Options and Issues*. Grand Rapids: Baker, 1995.
Gill, R. *A Textbook of Christian Ethics*. 2nd edition. Edinburgh: T&T Clark, 1995.
Gladwin, J. W. "Democracy." In *New Dictionary of Christian Ethics and Pastoral Theology*, edited by D. J. Atkinson, D. F. Field, A. F. Holmes, and O. O'Donovan, 294–295. Downers Grove: InterVarsity Press, 1995.
Goddard, B. L. "Joseph." *Baker's Dictionary of Theology*, edited by E. F. Harrison et. al. Grand Rapids: Baker Book House, 1960.
Grenz, S. J. *The Moral Quest*. Downers Grove: InterVarsity Press, 1997.
Haselbarth, Hans. *Christian Ethics in the African Context*. Ibadan: Daystar Press, 1976.
Heavenor, E. S. P. "Job." *New Bible Commentary Third Edition*, edited by J. D. Douglas. Leicester: Inter-Varsity Press, 1990.
Helm, P. "Kant, Immanuel." In *New Dictionary of Christian Ethics and Pastoral Theology*, edited by D. J. Atkinson, D. F. Field, A. F. Holmes, and O. O'Donovan, 55. Downers Grove: InterVarsity Press, 1995.
Henry, C. F. H. *Has Democracy Had Its Day?* Nashville: ERCC Publications, 1996.
Henry, M. *Matthew Henry's Commentary in One Volume: Genesis to Revelation*. Grand Rapids: Zondervan, 1961.
Hicks, P. A. "Truth." In *New Dictionary of Christian Ethics and Pastoral Theology*, edited by D. J. Atkinson, D. F. Field, A. F. Holmes, and O. O'Donovan, 867–868. Downers Grove: InterVarsity Press, 1995.
Hill, A. *Just Business*. Downers Grove: InterVarsity Press, 1997.
Holmes, A. F. *Ethics: Approaching Moral Decisions*. Leicester: Inter-Varsity Press, 1984.
Ibemere, E., and P. Oduenyi. "Rewarding Honesty." *The NEWS*. 6 October, 2003.
Kukah, M. H. *Democracy and Civil Society in Nigeria*. Ibadan: Spectrum Books, 2000.
Kunhiyop, S. W. *African Christian Ethics*. Kaduna: Baraka Press, 2004.
Lewis, J. "The Church and Formation of Political Conscience." *Review and Expositor* 73 (May 1976): 191–204.
Lindshell, H. Editor. *Harper Study Bible* (NASB). Grand Rapids: Zondervan, 1985.
Longman Dictionary of Contemporary English. London: Longman, 1978.

Luka, Reuben Turbi. *Jesus Christ as Ancestor.* Carlisle: Langham Monographs, 2019.
Maxwell, J. C. *Developing the Leader within You.* Nashville: Thomas Nelson, 1993.
Maxwell, J. C., and J. Dornan. *Becoming a Person of Influence.* Nashville: Thomas Nelson, 1997.
McGrath, A. E. "Sin and Salvation." In *New Dictionary of Christian Ethics and Pastoral Theology*, edited by D. J. Atkinson, D. F. Field, A. F. Holmes, and O. O'Donovan, 28. Downers Grove: InterVarsity Press, 1995.
McQuilkin, R. *An Introduction to Biblical Ethics.* 2nd edition. Wheaton: Tyndale House, 1995.
Microsoft® Encarta® 2009. © 1993–2008 Microsoft Corporation.
Mitchell, T. C. "Noah." *New Bible Dictionary*, edited by J. D. Douglas, N. Hillyer, and F. F. Bruce. 2nd edition. Leicester, UK: Inter-Varsity Press, 1982.
Murphy, J., and C. Murphy. *An International Minister's Manual.* Blue Jay: Hundred-Fold Press, 2002.
Nwankwo, A. A. *African Dictators.* Enugu: Fourth Dimension, 1990.
———. *Thoughts on Nigeria.* Enugu: Fourth Dimension, 1986.
Nwosu, N. I. "Political Leadership and Instability of the Nigerian State." In *Issues in Contemporary African Social and Political Thought*, vol. 2, edited by O. Obafemi and B. Lawal, 70–76. Lagos: Academic Publication, 1994.
Obaje, Y. A. *Theonicracy and Not Democracy for Nigeria.* Ogbomoso: Ogunniyi Publishers, 1994.
Obasanjo, O. *A New Dawn.* Abuja: PCU, 2000.
———. "New Year's Message-Broadcast on NTA, A New Dawn." Abuja: PCU, 2000.
———. *Nzeogwo.* Ibadan: Spectrum Books, 1987.
Obiechina, E. "Democracy Is Failing Again in Nigeria." *The Guardian.* Sunday January 23, 2005.
Ojiako, J. O. *13 Years of Military Rule.* Lagos: Daily Times of Nigeria, n.d.
Okolo, C. B. *Philosophy and Nigerian Politics.* Uruowulu-Obasi: Pacific College Press, 1985.
Olatunji, J. O. "Public, Accountability and Nation Building in Nigeria: 1993 and Beyond." In *Issues in Contemporary African Social and Political Thought*, vol. 2, edited by O. Obafemi and B. Lawal, 90–102. Lagos: Academic Publication, 1994.
Olugbade, K. "State of the State in the Third World." *Issues in Contemporary African Social and Political Thought*, vol. 2, edited by O. Obafemi and B. Lawal, 42–47. Lagos: Academia Publications, 1994.
Omoregbe, J. I. *Ethics.* Maryland: JOJA, 1993.
The Open Bible (NASB). Nashville: Thomas Nelson, 1985.
Osadolor, O. B. "The Development of the Federal Idea and the Federal Framework, 1914–1960." In *Federalism and Political Restructuring in Nigeria*, edited by K. Amuwo et al. Ibadan: Spectrum Books, 2003.
Otite, O., and W. Ogionwo. *Introduction to Sociological Studies.* Ibadan: Heinemann, 1985.

Oxford Advanced Learner's Dictionary of Current English. Ninth edition. Oxford: Oxford University Press, 2015.

Oyediran, O. *Introduction to Political Science*. Ibadan: Oyediran Consult International, 2003.

Ozodo, P. *Nigerian Covenant: Study Guide*. Jos: Covenant Keepers, 2001.

Palma, A. D. "Biblical Foundation." In *Church and Nationhood*, edited by B. J. Nicholls. New Delhi: World Evangelical Fellowship, 1978.

Patterson, C. H. *Moral Standards: An Introduction to Ethics*. New York: Ronald Press, 1949.

Reid, M. A. "Values, Value Judgments." In *New Dictionary of Christian Ethics and Pastoral Theology*, edited by D. J. Atkinson, D. F. Field, A. F. Holmes, and O. O'Donovan, 872. Downers Grove: InterVarsity Press, 1995.

Roberts, R. C. "Character." In *New Dictionary of Christian Ethics and Pastoral Theology*, edited by D. J. Atkinson, D. F. Field, A. F. Holmes, and O. O'Donovan, 65. Downers Grove: InterVarsity Press, 1995.

———. "Honesty." In *New Dictionary of Christian Ethics and Pastoral Theology*, edited by D. J. Atkinson, D. F. Field, A. F. Holmes, and O. O'Donovan, 454. Downers Grove: InterVarsity Press, 1995.

Sagay, I. "A Nation, Its Problems and Capable Leadership." *The Guardian*. Friday October 10, 2003.

Salamone, F. A. "Ethics Identities and Religion." In *Religion and Society in Nigeria*, edited by J. K. Olupona and T. Falola, 45–46. Ibadan: Spectrum Books, 1991.

Sangosanya, J. *Emirate Council and Politics in Northern Nigeria*. Jos: Niri Press, 2004.

Sani, H. A. "The Intellectual in Nation-Building: The Nigerian Experience." In *Issues in Contemporary African Social and Political Thought*, vol. 2, edited by O. Obafemi and B. Lawal, 126–127. Lagos: Academic Publication, 1994.

Schwarz, Jr., F. A. O. *Nigeria: The Tribes, the Nation, or the Race – The Politics of Independence*. Cambridge, MA: Massachusetts Institute of Technology Press, 1965.

Schwarz, W. *Nigeria*. London: Pall Mall Press, 1968.

Simmons, P. D. "Morality: Church and Government." *Review and Expositor* 73 (May 1976): 131–139. https://doi.org/10.1177/003463737607300202.

Singh, D. E. "Analysis of Mawlawa Mawdudi's Political Theory in the Context of Hindu-Muslim Relations in the Indian Sub-continent." *Religion and Society* 46 (March–June 1999): 123–127.

Soyinka, W. "Engaging the Past: Lessons from South Africa." *TELL*, May 17, 1999, 44.

Stock, Robert. "Nigeria." Microsoft® Encarta® 2009 [DVD]. Redmond, WA: Microsoft Corporation, 2008.

Storkey, A. "Materialism." In *New Dictionary of Christian Ethics and Pastoral Theology*, edited by D. J. Atkinson, D. F. Field, A. F. Holmes, and O. O'Donovan, 575–576. Downers Grove: InterVarsity Press, 1995.

Stott, John R. W. *The Contemporary Christian*. Leicester: Inter-Varsity Press, 2001.

———. "Human Rights and Human Wrongs: Major Issues for a New Century." Grand Rapids: Baker Books, 1999. https://www.kairosjournal.org/document.aspx?DocumentID=5150&QuadrantID=3&CategoryID=11&TopicID=27&L=1.
———. *Issues Facing Christians Today*. London: Harper Collins, 2006.
Strang, J. V. "Ethics as Politics: On Aristotelian Ethics and Its Contents." *The Paideia Archive: Twentieth World Congress of Philosophy* 3 (1998): 274–285. https://www.pdcnet.org/wcp20-paideia/content/wcp20-paideia_1998_0003_0274_0285.
Tamuno, T. N. "Nigerian Federalism in Historical Perspective." In *Federalism and Political Restructuring in Nigeria*, edited by K. Amuwo et al. 13–33. Ibadan: Spectrum Books, 1998.
Tidwell, J. B. *The Bible, Period by Period*. Nashville: Broadman Press, 1923.
Tillman, Jr., W. M. *Christian Ethics: A Primer*. Nashville: Broadman Press, 1986.
———, ed. *Understanding Christian Ethics*. Nashville: B&H Academic, 1988.
Tullock, J. H. *The Old Testament Story*. Englewood Cliffs: Prentice Hall, 1987.
Umar, A. "Politics." *The Guardian*. Sunday January 23, 2005.
Warren, R. *The Purpose Driven Life*. Grand Rapids: Zondervan, 2002.
Yamsat, P. *The Role of the Church in Democratic Governance in Nigeria*. Bukuru: Biblical Studies Foundation, 2002.
Yesufu, Momoh Lawani. "The Impact of Religion on a Secular State: The Nigerian Experience." http://www.scielo.org.za/scielo.php?script=sci_arttext&pid=S1017-04992016000100003.
Yoder, J. N. *The Politics of Jesus*. Grand Rapids: Eerdmans, 1994.

Langham Literature and its imprints are a ministry of Langham Partnership.

Langham Partnership is a global fellowship working in pursuit of the vision God entrusted to its founder John Stott –

> *to facilitate the growth of the church in maturity and Christ-likeness through raising the standards of biblical preaching and teaching.*

Our vision is to see churches in the Majority World equipped for mission and growing to maturity in Christ through the ministry of pastors and leaders who believe, teach and live by the word of God.

Our mission is to strengthen the ministry of the word of God through:
- nurturing national movements for biblical preaching
- fostering the creation and distribution of evangelical literature
- enhancing evangelical theological education

especially in countries where churches are under-resourced.

Our ministry

Langham Preaching partners with national leaders to nurture indigenous biblical preaching movements for pastors and lay preachers all around the world. With the support of a team of trainers from many countries, a multi-level programme of seminars provides practical training, and is followed by a programme for training local facilitators. Local preachers' groups and national and regional networks ensure continuity and ongoing development, seeking to build vigorous movements committed to Bible exposition.

Langham Literature provides Majority World preachers, scholars and seminary libraries with evangelical books and electronic resources through publishing and distribution, grants and discounts. The programme also fosters the creation of indigenous evangelical books in many languages, through writer's grants, strengthening local evangelical publishing houses, and investment in major regional literature projects, such as one volume Bible commentaries like *The Africa Bible Commentary* and *The South Asia Bible Commentary*.

Langham Scholars provides financial support for evangelical doctoral students from the Majority World so that, when they return home, they may train pastors and other Christian leaders with sound, biblical and theological teaching. This programme equips those who equip others. Langham Scholars also works in partnership with Majority World seminaries in strengthening evangelical theological education. A growing number of Langham Scholars study in high quality doctoral programmes in the Majority World itself. As well as teaching the next generation of pastors, graduated Langham Scholars exercise significant influence through their writing and leadership.

To learn more about Langham Partnership and the work we do visit **langham.org**

www.ingramcontent.com/pod-product-compliance
Lightning Source LLC
Chambersburg PA
CBHW070539170426
43200CB00011B/2479